Emotional Abuse & Trauma Recovery

How to Recognize, Overcome &
Heal from Psychological
Manipulation or Abuse & Build
Your Self-Esteem

Relove Psychology

FREE GIFT

Greetings!

First of all, we want to thank you for reading our books. We aim to create the very best books for our readers.

Now we invite you to join our exclusive list. As a subscriber, you will receive a free gift, weekly tips, free giveaways, discounts and so much more.

All of this is 100% free with no strings attached!

To claim your bonus simply head to the link below or scan the QR code below.

RELOVEPSYCHOLOGY

https://www.subscribepage.com/relovepsychology

CONTENTS

Trigger warning: This book contains references to emotional trauma and abuse that may be upsetting to some readers.

INTRODUCTION

Some scars don't hurt. Some scars are numb. Some scars rid you of the capacity to feel anything ever again —Joyce Rachelle

These words may strike a deeper chord with some of us, because our realities may sadly echo them.

Let me avoid adding to the mystery surrounding something that already lacks thorough understanding; I am referring to emotional abuse and trauma. And there will be no skirting around any of the aspects of these topics in this book. We are going to pull back the curtain, blow the lid, and reveal it for what it truly is. We will take it out of the mind's secret recesses, where all the invisible wounds accumulate, confront it, reflect on it, and consider ways to heal from it.

It is time to take off the mask you have been wearing for far too long; whether from childhood or adulthood, emotional abuse and trauma can come from a variety of sources in a variety of ways. It is not restricted to race, education, socioeconomic status, or religion. It is something that can occur to anyone at any time. Even if the wounds and scars are not physically visible, they can manifest in various ways, preventing you from living your best life possible.

Emotional abuse causes trauma and distress in its victims, leaving them hopeless and in a constant state of despair. This not only affects them physically, but it also has profound negative mental effects on its victims, as it does with all forms of abuse. To name a few disastrous examples, it erodes their joy, fulfillment, self-esteem, self-worth, and even life expectancy. And what kind of life is it if these fundamental rights are not guaranteed? Who has the authority to do something like this to another person?

Simply put, it is not a life; it has been hijacked, and you are no longer the captain of your ship. Who is to blame? Abusers; those with an insatiable desire for control, those who distort reality and lack empathy. To be honest, people with such tendencies are dangerous, and being in their presence is even more dangerous. They will drain your life force, leaving you a mere shadow of your former self, and you will find yourself isolated and living a false narrative. You are essentially a psychological hostage; your thoughts and judgments are not your own; your voice has been silenced, and your truth has been stolen.

This all sounds very surreal, does it not? However, this is the reality for many people.

There is a lot of awareness in society about physical abuse and how to combat it, as well as the importance of mental health. However, when it comes to emotional abuse, the same light is not shed on the dark, secretive, and traumatic world where victims of emotional abuse find themselves trapped. According to a study conducted with 250 participants that have been in a relationship for over a year, the effects of emotional abuse are just as severe as those of physical abuse (Karakurt & Silver, 2013). This makes it even more important to lift the veil and spread information about this often-overlooked aspect of abuse.

When it comes to abuse, just because you cannot physically prove it does not mean it does not exist. And it is precisely this small detail that makes it so difficult for victims of emotional abuse to reach out. Who would possibly believe me? How could I even begin to explain something that I do not fully comprehend? How do I bring this seemingly "invisible monster" to light?

This, dear reader, is precisely why I wrote this book. It is filled with information that will educate, motivate, and encourage you. You are not alone, and you are not to blame. It is time to expose this heinous truth and allow you to move on with your life. This is possible; you, like so many others, can overcome emotional abuse. You have the ability to transform like a butterfly, transitioning from victim to survivor by stepping into your beautiful self.

How are you going to accomplish this?

You have already begun; you are reading, educating yourself, arming yourself with strategies, and you are being courageous.

In this book, we will be exploring various aspects of emotional abuse, such as narcissistic tactics, codependency, and abandonment fears, to name a few. We will look in-depth at how these abusers use these heinous tactics to exert control, the consequences, and some solutions and strategies you can employ for each.

This will only be done to increase your understanding of the devil you are up against. But in the end, it is all about you and your recovery; for once in your life, it is not about them. So, another subject that we shall examine in depth is healing. You will be able to identify what is beneficial to your well-being and learn some steps you can take to reinforce your positive outlook on the world around you, as well as help reinforce a healthier perception of yourself.

It is time to emerge from the darkness of control and into the light of your own destiny. You are the author of your own story, and you have the power to change it. The delusions of grandeur that most abusers suffer from and enforce by instilling fear, control, and isolation, will no longer have a hold on you. Those days are long gone. With additional reading, you will be exposed to a wealth of information that will open your eyes to many truths that you have been forced to dismiss.

So, without further ado, let us get the ball rolling on your journey and healing process.

CHAPTER 1
EMOTIONAL ABUSE

You may have heard the famed "grin and bear it" adage. We have become accustomed to hearing that things are not always as bad as they seem. Surely, this has been proposed with good intentions, at least in most cases.

However, have you ever considered the significance of these words?

In actuality, oftentimes things are indeed as bad as they seem. Let us take this a step further; often, the bad things cannot be seen. That is a frightening concept, and for many, it is regrettably a harsh reality.

As much as we all live in a world that is full of beauty and things to be grateful for, there is darkness in our midst. We face challenges such as war, famine, violence, and abuse, to mention a few. These catastrophic situations all have the propensity to inflict significant trauma on our delicate human states, and for good reason: They are all akin to a living hell that is paired with an aftermath of severe detrimental proportions, whether it be physically, psychologically, or both. Most, if not all of us will undoubtedly come face-to-face with these challenges in some shape or form, walking away with the scars that serve as eternal reminders of what we have been through.

Yet what happens when you go through a challenge, experiencing the same trauma, feeling the same suffering, but walk away with no battle scar? On top of that, you feel the strain of pledged silence about what you have experienced, without being able to utter a word, and if you do, where is your verification?

I am referring to emotional abuse, a type of interaction that operates so far outside of any normal interpersonal dynamic that it is frequently incomprehensible.

Any sort of trauma leaves deeply entrenched wounds and scars in the minds and souls of its survivors, making any physical agony appear in a more preferred light.

Have you noted that I used the word survivor?

Anyone who has ever faced any type of trauma, physical or emotional, is a survivor because those scars that leave deep trenches in your heart are in actuality not that; they are medals, stars that shine from your heart and mind, and you are no longer a victim; you are a survivor.

Let us proceed and go deeper into the subject of

emotional abuse as our first step in order for you to get those stars all brilliant and sparkling in your head and heart, allowing you to proudly wear your survivor's status as you move from strength to strength.

Recognizing Abuse

Let us reveal this evil, exposing all of its masks, mannerisms, and maneuvers, enabling you to point it out and call it out without hesitation, even if it was as camouflaged and concealed as something in a "Where's Waldo" book.

Taking this into account, allow me to start from the top and guide the way down into this abyss because, contrary to what you have been led to believe, you are not alone, and together we shall expose every detail. There is no longer any time or reason for you to keep quiet about this. It is time to talk and allow that beautiful voice of yours to be heard.

What is Abuse?

You are undoubtedly familiar with the term abuse; nevertheless, awareness of the word predates awareness of many people experiencing abuse. I say this because, in many cases, people are unaware that they are being abused and exploited, and what makes matters worse is that abuse is not always observable.

Abuse happens when there is a behavioral pattern that arises when one person, the abuser, inflicts or projects purposeful, hurtful, and offensive behavior onto another, who is commonly referred to as the victim. The abuser's activities are not only physical in nature, but often take many different forms, making it difficult to detect and counter, especially when it comes to emotional or psychological abuse.

There are a startling number of various types of abuse, including some of the following:

- Physical abuse occurs when any sort of physical pain, resulting in injury, is perpetrated on a person, leaving bruises, wounds, broken bones, or even death, depending on the degree of the abuse.

- When a person's sexual boundaries and rights are broken, this is referred to as sexual abuse. This might involve both physical sexual wrongdoing, such as rape, and verbal sexual insults directed at another person.

- Elder abuse, as the name implies, occurs when senior individuals are abused, generally at the hands of their caregivers, and typically includes withholding food, water, and medicine, as well as other types of abuse such as physical or emotional offenses.

- Threats, insults, name-calling, humiliation, or any other type of disparaging remarks shouted or yelled at another person in order to exert control are examples of verbal abuse.

- Emotional abuse is what we will be honing in on in this book. This form of abuse is one of the most difficult to prove and often involves isolation, discrimination, control, as well as a significant amount of verbal abuse.

As a result, let us further deconstruct emotional abuse and the myriad ways this evil may manifest itself.

Types of Emotional Abuse

Due to the lack of physical injury, emotional and psychological abuse is sometimes disregarded, underestimated, and incorrectly dismissed as being less serious than physical abuse.

The fact that this form of abuse is extremely frequent and that society fails to acknowledge or address it exposes its victims to a slew of negative consequences, making it one of the most significant societal disasters of our time.

Allow me to begin by bringing to light the many types of emotional abuse to help make it simpler to spot, before we go on to a deeper knowledge of the impact this type of cruelty has on a person's life.

Name-Calling

Words have the potential to penetrate deeply into a person's soul and psyche, therefore name-calling is far from superficial. Targeting a person's sexuality, identity, or character, often disguised as a joke, name-calling is used as a method of manipulation and control.

Guilt

This refers to violating or making a person feel bad for setting and attempting to maintain their boundaries, oftentimes making the victim forget that boundaries are there to protect them and not hurt others.

Isolation

This is a real example of a wolf in sheep's clothing, in which the abuser convinces their victim that their friends and family do not care about their well-being, prompting them to disengage from and sever fundamental bonds, wrongly perceiving the abuser as the only true support in their lives. As a result, the victim becomes more susceptible and vulnerable to the abuser.

Overprotection

When it comes to emotional abuse, the fine line between being protective and being overprotective is repetitively crossed. Overprotectiveness is frequently the result of the abuser's jealousy, control, insecurity, possessiveness, or inferiority. This is typically characterized by the abuser projecting anger or humiliating conduct toward their victims' interactions and connections with others.

Gaslighting

Have you ever felt like you are losing your mind? Perhaps you felt like you are being crazy to feel the way you do, disregarding your emotions as odd. We all experience that from time to time; however, if another person makes you feel insecure and makes you question your own truth, you are being gaslighted. This terribly covert move can make victims feel that they should be grateful for the love and affection from their abuser because they see themselves as extremely undeserving and inferior.

Coercive Sex

Sex is an essential component of a healthy relationship; it should be joyful, but victims of emotional abuse are usually made to feel bad if they refuse to engage in sex. Because the victim is just cooperating to avoid emotional punishment, this guilt trip frequently leads to nonconsensual sex. In extreme cases, this can lead to rape and pregnancy coercion, increasing the person's internal trauma.

Stalking

When it comes to our personal lives and the onslaught of social media, monitoring apps, and smart gadgets, there is not much left to the imagination. As much as technology helps us in our everyday lives, it might also be a wonderful weapon for abusers' malevolent intentions, leaving victims with little privacy, forcing them to walk on eggshells and overthink every move and encounter, leading them to live in a perpetual state of subconscious anxiety.

Cold-Shouldering

This type of passive and hostile action is used to

disregard the victim themselves. It is one of the most typical ways that abusers subject their victims to psychological torture, making them feel unheard and invisible, which is generally accompanied by feelings of guilt, vulnerability, and humiliation on the victim's part.

Destruction of Property

This involves the abuser physically acting out, whether by throwing things around, breaking objects, or punching holes in walls and doors, as a demonstration of their wrath, and terror tactics. Although the damage is done to tangible items, the concern is that it might swiftly escalate into physical violence.

Financial Abuse

This is a type of manipulation in which control is exercised by limiting the victim's capacity to access or control funds. This may be achieved by limiting the victim's access to money and resources, preventing them from working, and requiring them to get permission before making purchases. It becomes harder for the victim to leave the abusive relationship because of how reliant they are on the abuser.

Body Shaming

Body shaming is another strategy used by abusers to make their victims feel unsightly, undeserving, and worthless, causing a significant drop in their self-esteem and self-image. This is closely similar to name-calling, in which physical characteristics are called out and appraised negatively, leading victims to feel that no one else finds them beautiful, entrapping them in the relationship out of fear.

Sleep Deprivation

Many abusers keep their victims up at night, preventing them from maintaining stable, healthy sleeping habits. Knowing how crucial sleep is for mind and body regeneration, not getting enough sleep can result in victims suffering memory loss, irritability, and brain fog. This adds fuel to the fire of self-doubt, which is already a major component of emotional abuse.

We are only skimming the surface here since abusers will go to any length to feel as if they have complete control over their victims; therefore, adopting various strategies is rather common with people who enact emotional abuse. Couples or partners are not the only ones capable of establishing a master-servant hierarchy, emphasizing their demands while ignoring yours. Relationships with parents, caregivers, business partners, and adult children can all exhibit this dynamic. Let us recap, any action or strategy that causes the following in any way, shape, or form, should raise red flags and warrant greater scrutiny:

- humiliation
- negation
- criticism
- control
- accusation

- denial
- neglect
- isolation

Being exposed to emotional abuse is a traumatic experience in and of itself, opening the floodgates to a slew of harmful consequences; we will focus on these next because being able to detect them also plays a key part in recognizing emotional abuse.

What Is the Impact?

The intriguing aspect of emotional abuse is that it is not just the abuser's dark side that causes fissures in their victims, but also the fact that their moods fluctuate from loving, fun, and romantic to darker moods. This generates bewilderment and insecurity, which further exacerbates the fissures. As a result, it is a collection of the good, bad, and ugly and how these abusers play them out and subject their victims to these experiences and moods.

Let us have a closer look at the impacts emotional abuse has on the lives of so many that are subjected to it.

Short-Term Impacts

When you begin to realize that you may be a victim of emotional abuse, being in denial is a natural reaction; after all, what you are doing is trying to make sense of a nonsensical situation that you have been subjected to. You could feel:

- fear
- shame
- confusion
- hopelessness

And, as we all know, emotions present themselves in a variety of physical manifestations, which means you could also be experiencing some of the following symptoms:

- physical aches, pains, and muscular tension
- nightmares and sleep disturbances
- mood fluctuations
- an accelerated heart rate
- difficulty concentrating and remaining focused
- feeling overwhelmed

Unfortunately, this is not where it ends, these impacts can leave long-term scars because in general, this form of abuse occurs over long periods of time.

Long-Term Impacts

Do not be deceived into thinking that since you have no visible wounds, the effects of emotional abuse should be ignored. You do have wounds, and they run deep. It has been established that the repercussions of mental abuse are just as devastating as those of physical abuse (Karakurt & Silver, 2013).

Long-term consequences of emotional abuse may include the following:

- depression
- low self-esteem

- guilt
- insomnia
- chronic fatigue syndrome
- chronic pain
- anxiety
- loneliness, isolation, and social withdrawal
- Fibromyalgia
- Post-traumatic stress disorder (PTSD)

As you can see, these effects have a far-reaching impact on a person's life, leading to a life that is only half-fulfilled, which no one deserves. We all deserve to live our best possible lives.

Healing From Abuse

It is critical to not only be able to identify abuse but also take action to recover from it and live the happy, fulfilled life that you deserve.

One of the first initial phases in the healing process is the ability to digest the information. As the saying goes: The first step towards solving a problem is admitting that there is one.

Because healing and recovery from emotional abuse is such a personal process to go through, what works for one person may not necessarily work for another. Regardless of how your healing and recovery occur, the crucial thing to remember is that it is not your fault, it is not okay, and you are under no obligation to ever live with any form of abuse.

Another crucial thing to remember, no matter how

lonely you may feel, is that you are not alone. So many individuals suffer in silence at the hands of an emotional abuser and realize that speaking up and reaching out is a means to empower not only themselves but also others by serving as a voice and source of inspiration for everyone. There are also support groups that help those who are going through the same thing; there are friends and family, counselors, and therapists; all you have to do is take the first step and reach out. And believe me when I say that you will be pleasantly surprised at how many people understand, care, and are prepared to provide you with much-needed support.

As you take that first step toward emotional freedom, here are some guidelines that could help you persevere

Build a Strong Support Network
This may be a frightening concept at first, but it is vital and plays a critical part in your rehabilitation. As previously said, having a solid support system will not only assist in your healing but will also accelerate the process.

Leave the Relationship
Being in an abusive relationship is not the same as having a partnership; it is a hostage situation, and remaining with someone who abuses you is tantamount to inflicting a life sentence on yourself. To heal from the experience, you must separate yourself

from the crisis and the cause, which entails severing all ties.

You Cannot Fix Them

You have no power to change others; you only have the power to change yourself. Oftentimes a victim hopes and wishes that the abuser will change. It is not completely impossible, but it is not your objective; your healing is. If they wish to change, they should make the decision and take the required actions by obtaining professional help.

Prioritize Your Needs

Setting boundaries, reaching out to others, and leaving the source are the best things you can do for yourself. Your physical and mental well-being should take precedence; get back on the wagon and recognize your value.

Block and Ignore

Visualize the following words etched out in bright neon letters in the sky: Avoid engaging with them! Emotional abusers are master manipulators, so steer clear. This includes no phone calls, texts, emails, or other forms of communication. If you are in a circumstance where you cannot avoid severing all links, because you are sharing a kid or working in the same office, make sure to always have another person in your presence when communicating with the person who is emotionally abusing you and confine the conversation to the bare necessities.

Set Healthy Boundaries

It is vital to establish and convey appropriate, healthy boundaries. Remember that these are meant to protect you, not to offend others, so know when and where to draw the line, especially when you are getting drawn into emotionally abusive vortexes. It is critical that you adhere to these boundaries; they should never be bargained or gambled with; they are unchangeable.

Stop the Blame Game

Working with feelings of shame and blame that have arisen as a result of the abuse is a difficult thing to grasp at times. Remember, no one deserves to be abused. Regardless of what they lead you to think, the only one culpable is the abuser. Remember that much, if not most, of what they told you to believe was simply part of their calculated control tactics and does not deserve to take up any further precious real estate in your head and heart.

Be Patient

Be gentle and patient with yourself, healing is not something that occurs overnight. You need to relearn who you are as a person to reset a lot of the damaging patterns that have been ingrained in you. Give yourself some time; it will be worthwhile.

As it is one of, if not the most essential, aspects of abuse, we will be looking more closely at the connection between emotional abuse and the healing process in subsequent chapters.

As a result of your improved comprehension of the fundamentals of emotional abuse, you will be better able to recognize these basic patterns. In this case, knowledge is truly power since it will help you shed light on these troubling circumstances and direct you toward making wiser judgments for yourself.

Let us continue on our path and examine narcissistic abuse recovery.

CHAPTER 2
NARCISSISTIC ABUSE RECOVERY

Oh, the bewilderment, the self-doubt that keeps creeping in and mucking with your "marbles" while you have a deep-seated knowledge that you did nothing wrong. Even though you are still trying to figure out what went wrong or what you might do or could have done differently to stop the abusive emotional agony.

Could you have taken a different action to influence the circumstance differently? Could you not have assisted your abuser in changing their mindset and strategy to avoid all of this?

In a nutshell: no. You could not; this is a common symptom of abuse and a dead giveaway that you are or were in a toxic relationship. Because of the intoxicating nature of these sorts of relationships, therapist Ellen Biros notes that toxic relationships have many similarities to addiction (Raypole, 2020). This is because, similar to addiction, there is reinforcement coupled with guilt and shame, which still plays a role during your recovery journey.

What does this seem like in layman's terms?

Because abusive relationships are traumatic, rehabilitation takes time, and the mind cycles back and forth, revisiting memories during this process. This creates some conflict between your comprehension of the abuse and the nice experiences you had with the person. The next thing you know, you are missing them and that familiarity, desiring their attention, and you maybe even become eager to give it another go.

You can bet your bottom dollar that those who perpetrate emotional abuse are well aware of this little feature over here and will most frequently be calmly waiting, ready to pounce at the slightest signals of you wavering in your judgment.

Thus, let us concentrate on these narcissistic abuse tactics.

Tactics to Control

Simply defined, narcissistic techniques used to gain control are cruel, calculated, and cold. Narcissists like distorting, deceiving, and sowing doubt, going to profound lengths, often at the expense of others.

These adept brainwashers lack empathy and honesty, and breaking free will necessitate you to develop your own sense of calculation.

And how does one intend to approach this?

Simply using your rational reflection and educating yourself on the tactics that narcissists use, can help you recognize the distortions that are being presented to you. Thus let us have a closer look at their bag of tricks.

Projection

This is one of the most obvious indicators that you are dealing with a narcissist. Projection is the narcissist accusing others of doing what they are truly accountable for.

They would label you a liar if they are the liar, and you may be informed that you are untrustworthy, while the truth is that they should not be trusted. You may be labeled as being manipulative, and guess what? They are the ones who are manipulating. This might be anything from rage to laziness, even abuse. I am confident that if you take a moment to contemplate, you will be able to resonate.

Narcissists are often hypocritical and employ this method to evade accountability for their acts and attitudes, and the worst thing is that they actually believe these falsehoods.

Badgery

They have no difficulty putting you under strain by blasting you with questions, comments, and demands.

This is due to their attitude of entitlement and their inability to see how obnoxious they appear to others. You may feel pressed to respond quickly, or pressured to make rapid judgments, and they will continue to press you until you surrender.

They often repeat information, especially lies, assuming that doing so makes it true, and when it comes to hearing what others have to say and considering their perspectives, the request is only met with hostility and annoyance.

Shaming

Those who are described as "talented leaders" at tearing people down are often, in fact, narcissists. In truth, they harbor a deep-seated sense of shame, which is something they are not even conscious of.

What do they do about the nagging shame that is encroaching on them? Yes, they project; it is one of their favorite party tricks; they also judge, have strong opinions, and cast doubt on the sincerity of others. They elevate themselves above others in this way to feel better about themselves.

Flattery

Flattery is alright, but when it comes to narcissists you should never take their flattery to heart. They enjoy being showered with accolades, but they also use it as a form of control to obtain what they want.

They may merely flatter you in order to earn a compliment. This strategy might also be used to acquire what they want or to make and break you as they see fit to establish a sense of dependence on them.

Compliments might also be freely distributed as a form of deflection to escape accountability.

They adore this tactic but bear in mind that when it comes to narcissists and compliments, most are false flattery, there are ill motivations hiding behind those kind words.

Infantilizing

Talking down to people or addressing them in a childish, condescending tone is a tactic employed by narcissists to belittle others, making themselves feel superior. It is rather common for them to treat individuals as though they are of inferior intelligence to themselves.

Painting Your Reality

Narcissists truly suffer from grandiose illusions, believing they are oracles of some sort by identifying and depicting the reality of others.

Have you ever been told that no one knows you better than they do? Bingo!

All of this is done to confuse you and make you doubt yourself. They have no qualms about self-righteously categorizing the ideas, intentions, and feelings of others.

Explosive and Exaggerated Reactions

When it comes to regulating powerful emotions and urges, narcissists tend to slip up. Another tactic they use to gain the upper hand is to throw tantrums or act out explosively, which puts their victims on the defensive and gives them the advantage once more.

Playing it Down

A narcissist being wrong? Never, well, they are, but you have a higher chance of discovering a mermaid or "chicken teeth" than having a narcissist accept and acknowledge their transgressions.

They are masters of deflection; transferring responsibility, hiding behind denial, and rationalizing excuses are all part of their repertoire. They downplay their offenses, making it difficult for their victims to stand up to them.

Narcissism is a personality disorder (Arzt, 2022), and the hard fact is that while change is possible for everyone, it is exceedingly improbable for these people. People who have this personality disorder cannot stand being wrong, inferior, illegitimate, or humiliated. That is why they use these strategies to preserve their sense of superiority. This risky game comes at a high cost: The emotional welfare of others.

If you find yourself in a relationship where the other person takes a win-lose or right-wrong attitude rather than pursuing a win-win situation to create a fair playing field for all parties involved, you are dealing with a narcissist. Keep a look out for a frivolous emphasis on appearance rather than content, persuasion rather than honesty, and supremacy rather than equality.

Recognizing Narcissistic Abuse

Now that you understand how they play the game, let us examine how to spot when you are up against a narcissist to further educate and equip you with the information you need to avoid being drawn into a warped reality.

We have examined the many forms of emotional abuse, thus you will already be familiar with the warning signals you should watch out for when it comes to recognizing narcissistic abuse. Some of the instances from our earlier discussion include gaslighting, manipulation, and verbal abuse, but they are all equivalent to narcissistic abuse. The second thing to be aware of is the person's behavioral habits; narcissists will often project the following traits:

- envy
- jealousy
- entitlement
- arrogance
- need for admiration
- attention-seeking behavior
- delusions of grandeur and superiority
- overt charisma

I would like to present you with a new piece of information: the abuse cycle, also known as the narcissistic abuse cycle. Though narcissists feel they are unique, brilliant, and superior to others, they are actually rather predictable. If you recognize the tactics, traits, and cycle, you may find yourself seeing the wider picture and chuckling at the predictable repetition, which in reality lacks absolute creativity.

The Narcissistic Abuse Cycle

This cycle can be used to aid those who are suffering at the hands of a narcissist by forming part of their awareness.

However, it is important to state that the National Domestic Violence Hotline contends that including the idea of a cycle could make this kind of abuse seem predictable, and some victims would feel as though they should know what is intended to happen next, causing them to blame themselves for any occurrences ("Is Abuse Really a "Cycle?", n.d.).

So, bear in mind that this is not a forecast; rather, it is a cycle intended to shed light on a behavioral pattern, and noting this latter perspective is vital to avoid choosing an approach in which you believe you should have known better. Abuse is not your fault, end of story. We cannot predict the future, but we can educate ourselves to the best of our ability.

Idealization

Abusers first appear to be the nicest people and perfect companions, incredibly charming, enamored, and alluring. This all adds up to a strong concoction that leads the victim to believe that this may be a match made in heaven.

Devaluation

Then, the "honeymoon" phase is over and cracks manifest as abuse. This does not happen right away; rather, it happens progressively as it builds up over time. For instance, it could begin as regular jealousy and evolve into verbal or gaslighting forms of abuse. The likelihood that this will keep growing is the cause for concern.

Rejection

Rejection is a narcissist's victim's greatest initial dread; this generally occurs when the narcissist is asked to make a compromise, comprehend, or change of perspective. And that is something that should not be expected.

This can happen all at once or in smaller, spaced-out episodes throughout the course of the relationship when you get love-bombed by the narcissist to boost you up before you unexpectedly come crashing down. This is what exacerbates the uncertainty and self-doubt.

Recovering From Narcissistic Abuse

Dr. Mike Dow, a highly experienced psychotherapist who works with people who have experienced emotional abuse, explains that narcissists prey on empathetic, sensitive people and suggests asking yourself a few simple questions to determine whether you need to begin the healing process from narcissistic abuse (Loggins, 2021).

These are some of the questions:

- Am I getting my needs met in this relationship on a consistent basis?
- In all honesty, am I being manipulated and my needs being ignored?
- Do I suspect that I am being manipulated but turn a blind eye to it?
- Do I find myself constantly sacrificing my own needs and relationships in order to serve and make this person happy?

Answering yes to most of these questions is a strong indicator that you should begin making significant adjustments to reclaim your true happiness and live a fulfilled life. But thankfully there are methods that could help you in your journey to start healing from narcissistic abuse. Let us look at some below.

Name It

Labeling abuse is challenging, but being able to identify what has happened and call it out for what it is, empowers you to have a sense of objectivity toward the issue. This is significant because objectivity is eroded when you are continuously thrust between a narcissist's charm and their cruelty.

End It

As previously said, it is critical to entirely distance yourself from the source of abuse; any form of improvement concerning the relationships is tantamount to wishful thinking.

Set It

Yes, this is yet again all about those very important boundaries you should set in place and never ever tamper with in order to protect yourself. This will assist you to avoid or restrict contact, as well as any engagement involving narcissistic retribution.

You Need It

Support is an essential component of any recovery process following abuse. It is critical to reach out and establish a robust support system or network of trustworthy, high-quality folks who have your best interests at heart. This could include family, friends, support groups, professional counseling, or a combination of these.

Schedule It

Developing a healthy routine can assist you in remaining focused on what is essential in your recovery journey. It is not always simple to stick to a schedule, but routines are also not fixed in stone. Rather, they act as a guide that might provide you with a sense of control, especially when you feel scattered and bewildered.

Anticipate It

It is critical to be realistic when grieving what you have gone through. Ending a relationship is a form of loss, it is a traumatic experience for anyone. Allowing yourself to experience the complicated emotions that are associated with grief, such as numbness, longing, and difficulty keeping up with daily tasks, is an essential part of the healing process. This will subside with time and is a common occurrence that has to be navigated, thus be patient with yourself.

Express It

You will almost certainly feel as though you are drowning in a sea of emotions. Do not keep it pent up inside; get it off your chest and release your thoughts and feelings. If you do not want to talk about it, channel it by being creative, keeping a journal, or even taking up some physical activity.

Rediscover and Forgive It

Do not be surprised if you find yourself confused about who you are after leaving a narcissistic relationship. You have, after all, been projected onto and instructed what to believe, how to behave, and whom to see. Make a list of things you want to accomplish, consider what would make you truly happy and fulfilled, and then pursue those things. Spend time looking after yourself to make the process of self-discovery smoother; for instance, join a reading club or a fitness class. It is important to establish your own sense of importance again. The world is at your feet, and you have every right to seek out things that fulfill your needs.

As part of self-care, practice forgiveness. There is no point in blaming yourself for the bad decisions and behaviors of others, it will only stunt your healing, nobody deserves to be abused. Practice compassion, not just towards yourself but towards others, this will help you with regards to establishing a sense of self, as compassion is one of the major elements that is a no-show when it comes to a narcissistic relationship.

Protect It

Keep your emotions and privacy safeguarded. Be careful of what you post online, and be sure to delete and block the narcissist. Since there are many ways for others to probe into your life through social media, this does not completely secure your safety and privacy; nonetheless, it will limit their ability to do so and make it more difficult for them to re-enter your life.

Protecting yourself often entails putting the brakes on the dating scene as well. To begin recovering, you must first process what has happened to you, identify how narcissism impacts you, and rediscover who you are. Reentering the dating environment and going through the same agony is the last thing you want to do.

Reflect on It

Reflection is vital, but there is a fine line between thinking back on your prior interactions with narcissists and becoming fully obsessed with the pain they have caused you. It is important to remember that reflection also calls on you to take stock of your own accomplishments, growth, and lessons gained by looking back on your own strengths.

More time should be spent considering your positive traits since doing so will help you escape the narcissistic delusion you have fallen into.

One of the most difficult things to do is admit there is a problem, no matter what that problem is. When it comes to acknowledging that you are in a narcissistic relationship, accepting that you have been manipulated can be a hard pill to swallow.

Remember, your love and compassion are not to blame; the problem is the other party's abuse, and being deceived may happen to anybody. Recognizing the problem is essential, but moving on from there is much greater since that is when life will begin anew for you.

Next, we will look into gaslighting, a term that has recently gained prominence on the internet with people flinging it around every status, but what does this term essentially entail?

CHAPTER 3
GASLIGHTING

Although the phrase "gaslighting" has garnered some notoriety in recent years, the practice is not new. The phrase is based on the 1938 play Gaslight, in which a husband deceives his wife into believing she has a mental illness (Degges-White, 2022). It seems very horrible and harsh, would you not agree?

The reality is that this is a prevalent issue for many individuals, and this terrible form of abuse is not limited to romantic or personal relationships—any connection is susceptible. Gaslighting is a covetous kind of abuse when the victim loses their sense of identity and self-worth and is forced to live a lie. This is not some voodoo, it happens as a result of the abuser's manipulation, which makes the victim doubt their own judgment; setting off a wave of perplexity and unease.

In this dark world, abusers would do whatever it takes to undermine and destroy the core beliefs of a victim, twisting the facts, using crucial words like "love," impregnating them with evil purposes, lying, and utilizing passive aggression. They can employ any number of tactics and make several attempts to exert control over another person, just as with any other kind of abuse.

In order for you to better comprehend the mechanisms underlying this phenomenon that causes some individuals to feel as though their lives are stranger than fiction, let us briefly enter this realm and explore them.

Grasping Gaslighting

You would not even know that you have met a gaslighter, the relationship starts off pretty standard, as a matter of fact, everything starts fairly well.

You could be praised and confided in, which is all part of gaining your trust, the enticing tactic, commonly referred to as "love bombing", and generally lacking any signs of abuse. This makes it tricky to quickly slap a label on and identify a gaslighter.

When you are enthralled, the person who is gaslighting you is set to go on to the next stage, in which your own judgment and self-trust are gradually eroded, increasing your reliance on the gaslighter or abuser. It is a slow, deliberate procedure, similar to that of a frog in boiling water. Their words might be suggestive of you being forgetful, untrustworthy, or taking stabs at your mental stability. With time, these consistently planted seeds begin to form a mental pattern in your mind, causing you to believe that these lies are reality. Voila, just like that, the gaslighter has acquired authority and power.

From there, it tends to snowball to the point where you are so reliant that recalling memories, making decisions, or even questioning your judgment all require validation from the gaslighter, making you feel as if living without this person is nearly impossible.

That is how the false narrative is born, and you are like a butterfly stuck in a web spun with lies.

Recognizing Gaslighting

This is not normal conduct, and for someone to find it in themselves to be able to do this to someone else, something must be awry.

People who exhibit this type of conduct are likely to have a psychiatric problem of some kind, such as narcissistic personality disorder, psychopathy, or personality disorder. They wear many masks, and behind closed doors, that mask slips off, allowing them to focus on their victims in stark contrast to the masquerade they display in public. This is a challenge that many victims encounter; how could such a wonderful person be guilty of such atrocities? This aspect makes it difficult to speak out against this form of abuse.

As previously said, it is a snowball effect; the falsehoods begin small and seemingly innocent, with the odd positive reinforcement thrown in for good measure, maintaining a continuous level of toxicity. They sow doubt in everyone's minds, informing the victim, their friends, and their family that the victim has mental problems and is susceptible to delusions.

If you can resonate with any of the following, you should be concerned:

- Doubting your own feelings and truth.
- Feelings of vulnerability and insecurity.
- Feeling helpless, alienated, and lonely.
- Constantly challenging your own perceptions and conclusions.
- Experiencing issues with your self-esteem and sense of self.
- Feelings of self-disappointment as well as the belief that you continuously fail others.
- Feeling worried about being too sensitive.
- Confusion and a tendency to second-guess oneself.
- Feeling insecure and apologizing constantly, whether for who you are or what you do.
- Constantly doubting yourself and attempting to figure out what is wrong with you.
- Making any decision is difficult due to self-doubt.
- Feeling constantly on edge or threatened, as though no situation, person, or even you yourself can be trusted.

Any of these signs require you to reach out for help as the depth of psychological wounds can truly run deep and leave scars that take significant time to heal.

All of these emotions are elicited by manipulation tactics such as:

- lying
- minimizing
- denying
- distracting
- blaming
- false positive reinforcement

Let us put all of this information into context by considering a few real-life scenarios.

Gaslighting in Different Scenarios

As the gaslighter, gaslighting can be camouflaged in a variety of ways. Many of them appear to be typical actions that we encounter daily; nonetheless, they are consistent, forming a pattern and therefore a continual presence that steadily brainwashes victims over time.

Withholding

One of the most effective methods that gaslighters use to develop self-doubt is to pretend that they do not comprehend what is being said or to refuse to listen. For example:

- "You are quite confusing."
- "I have no idea what you are on about right now."

Countering

Your memory is under siege here. Questions and

statements are posed that induce you to doubt what you recall.

- "I think you might be forgetting some details."
- "Are you a hundred percent sure that is what happened?"

Stereotyping

Gaslighters, according to the American Sociological Review, usually use unfavorable preconceptions about a person's sexuality, age, color, gender, ethnicity, or culture to light that fire and gaslight them (Sweet, 2019).

- "Nobody would believe that coming from a woman."
- "That is to be expected from folks like you."

Trivializing

The major goal of the game here is to belittle and dismiss victims, making them feel as though they are too sensitive and overreacting if they respond to legitimate concerns.

- "You are simply being sensitive now; it was all a joke."
- "Do you really have to go this far and exaggerate everything?"

Denial

There is no arguing with these types of folk simply playing the denial card, yet again, casting doubt or blame. This is a method they employ to evade responsibility for their actions.

- "You must be imagining things, I did not say that at all."
- "You are making things up again to suit yourself."

Diversion

Your credibility is targeted here, and this is frequently used as a distraction strategy to divert attention away from themselves.

- "What were you read   ing? It is nonsense."
- "What are you thinking listening to things like that?"

They lack empathy; they may put on a performance to give the impression that they are empathic, but a gaslighter is incapable of doing so; instead, they see it as a chance to capitalize on your concerns. When you reveal any sign of vulnerability, you are essentially gift-wrapping a set of narcissistic tools for them to use to further erode your belief in yourself.

Gaslighters love the power they have over their victims, and whether or not they realize or verbalize their activities, their level of self-awareness is in no way a defense for their heinous deeds.

Dealing With and Recovering From Gaslighting

This is a control tool used by cult leaders and tyrants alike, not just domestic abusers.

You have a higher chance of spotting a gaslighter if you recognize the traits of the individuals who fall victim to their abuse; they are incredibly elusive and cunning, masquerading as the nicest people you could possibly meet. Of course, they are; otherwise, how would they entice their victims?

They keep their victims hooked by posing as the victim or using their bogus positive reinforcement strategy. They will go to any length without consideration for the impact it will have on their victim. As a result, do not anticipate any apology, admission of guilt, or genuine emotions. If you are fortunate enough to evade this fate, do not anticipate any sorrow; they will simply move on to their next victim.

The essential thing to remember is that you have the ability to put your foot down and heal from this form of abuse. It is your human right to live your best life. Next, we will look at some actions you may take to recover from gaslighting below.

Call It Out

Once more, perceive it for what it is and label it. Being able to describe what you are feeling is a really useful technique in the recovery process because you are essentially acknowledging that you are aware of what is happening to you and reclaiming your view of reality.

Break Free From It

As with any form of abuse, you must distance yourself from the perpetrator. You are essentially their source, and leaving their atmosphere will suffocate the abuse directed at you. They will always use strategies to make you question yourself and your decisions to maintain control, or they may just move on to their next source of supply. They are energy vampires that know how to get under your skin; thus, make sure to seek support and take the appropriate precautions. If you cannot avoid them, limit your contact with them and make sure you are never alone in any particular place or circumstance with them. They are perilous and will strike at any opportunity.

Write It Down

Keeping a record of your experiences is one of the most beneficial things you can do. Write down what happened, how you felt, and what you were thinking. Were you worried or perplexed? Do you get the feeling that something is amiss but you cannot put your finger on it? Write everything down, including the time, date, your feelings, and what was said and done. This may be used to not only reflect on what you have been through or felt but also to help you comprehend your sentiments and prove to yourself that they are valid when doubts arise. It may also help you regain faith in yourself, giving you the confidence to make adjustments and leave the environment.

Assert It

Enough is enough, and you must put your foot down and be assertive to communicate that they do not have that kind of authority over you, and you are not digesting and accepting all that they say; it is not law. Be responsive instead of reactive, you may say:

- "No, I did not say that; do not distort it."
- "I am not interested in continuing this topic."
- "You do not appear to be hearing me or understanding what I am saying."
- "You appear to be having difficulty comprehending something from a different perspective."

You might just say what you want to say and go without waiting around for a response. The best course of action after that is to confide in someone about what happened in order to establish your reality and help you remain grounded.

Do Not Argue It

These individuals are experts at argumentation and manipulating others. They are seasoned liars and are not worthy of engaging in any debate. They will impose their views on you, be the last arbiter, and make no effort to understand your point of view. You would have more success pulling anything out of a rock than arguing with a gaslighter. There is only one way, and that is their truth.

Remain Confident, Your Reality Is It

It is rather common to have trouble remembering certain details, especially minute ones like color, but it is far more difficult for your mind to make up and misremember complete memories. Additionally, because everyone remembers things differently, you could occasionally doubt your perspective and contrast it with that of others. The key distinction is in doubting your own reality because someone else is trying to make you question your whole world. Simply state again that you do, in fact, recall what happened and that you have no desire to further discuss it, then leave the room or bring up a different topic.

Check It

Being a gaslighter is telling pathological falsehoods without flinching and presenting them as if they are entire facts. Worse, most of the time gaslighters believe their lies, and when confronted with them, you may anticipate infuriated defensiveness. Verify the information on your own, do some fact-checking, if it is your actions that are put under fire, talk to a trusted friend or counselor or write it down in your journal, and perhaps later you can connect the dots. Find and fight for your own truth.

Talk About It

With any form of abuse, you need to reach out and talk about it. Do not overestimate the value of forming a strong, supporting network around yourself. Isolation is a powerful tool that all mental and emotional abusers employ. Reaching out and receiving support is undoubtedly a powerful strategy to counteract this deceitful behavior. This will also help you stay anchored in your reality since you will be able to authenticate your truth with those who care about your well-being rather than being lost in a world of fabrications.

As dark and deadly as these actions are, abusers' minds are very predictable; if you grasp their aim, which is ultimately control, you will also have a better understanding of the ways they use to achieve this, therefore being better equipped to safeguard your vital mental health and navigate these situations.

Let us proceed and arm you with more information to better prepare you to avoid these pitfalls.

CHAPTER 4
CODEPENDENCY

Relationships of any kind are all about giving and receiving, but there is a fine line to walk when it comes to this dynamic, and crossing it may mean the difference between a healthy and unhealthy relationship.

Dependency is an essential component of relationships; we need to feel wanted as well as be able to rely on others. Forming connections necessitates sharing information as well as being open and vulnerable to the views and feelings of others, resulting in exclusive attachments.

Codependency occurs when the scales of a relationship are tipped to the extreme, resulting in an unhealthy, dysfunctional, one-sided affair in which two separate roles; the giver and the receiver, are established.

Let us take a deeper look at this conundrum, also known as relationship addiction, which is another factor in abusive relationships.

Codependency and Its Roots

This is not restricted to romantic relationships and might wreak havoc on any connection, whether family, friends, or business.

According to The American Psychological Association (2022), codependency can be defined as a state of mutual reliance and a dysfunctional relationship pattern in which one party is dependent on or controlled by another party who has some form of a pathological condition such as substance abuse or any other form of addiction.

A codependent relationship requires mental, physical, spiritual, and emotional dependency from all parties involved. This type of reliance is undesirable because it lacks a fair playing field, the provider and taker scenario, which is analogous to master and servant or winner and loser. This is hardly a win-win situation.

This word found its origins in the world of addiction, initially appearing among circles of individuals who are dependent on substances of some sort, in this case, alcohol in particular, depicting a dynamic in which one party's addiction consumes and produces an imbalance in a relationship ("Codependency", 2022). As a result, this is a rather common occurrence in partnerships where one party struggles with addiction of any kind. This imbalance, which is not restricted to partnerships with addiction issues, places one person in the role of being the continuous caregiver, but not in a healthy way. The role of facilitator or enabler is a better term to define this caregiving persona. I am saying this because, in codependent relationships, being helpful and compassionate really enables the taker's harmful or negative conduct. In abusive relationships, this could be constantly taking blame or making excuses for the abuser's behavior for example.

People who play the role of the facilitator tend to have traits like people-pleasing, poor self-esteem, or insufficient boundaries, which makes them vulnerable to falling into this role. Although it overlaps with other personality disorders like dependent personality disorder and incorporates attachment style traits that are often acquired in childhood, codependency is not a clinical illness.

Relying on someone in a relationship does not imply that you are codependent; as previously said, good partnerships contain some degree of reliance, which is referred to as an interdependent relationship. Both sides' needs are addressed and satisfied, and they may still pursue their own interests and hobbies outside of the partnership. The master-servant dynamic is non-existent since interdependent relationships are defined by mutual respect, value, and love shared by both parties.

How Does This Happen?

According to Dr. Mark Mayfield, a licensed professional counselor, weak self-concept, the inability to say no, the inability to establish and have ideas, and inadequate boundaries are all factors that come into play with codependency (Gould, 2022).

These characteristics are common in those who have experienced trauma or dysfunctional family relationships, such as growing up with a family member who suffered from addiction or some form of mental illness. This is often associated with feelings of insecurity, fear, shame, anger, and anxiety, which are then projected and expected with any type of connection.

Codependency is not restricted to persons who have these qualities or come from these backgrounds; anybody can descend into destructive relationship patterns, thus none of us are "immune" to having these encounters. I should stress that abuse is not the victim's fault and that anybody can fall victim to it.

Codependency is known to take many forms, and research has divided it into social, biological, and psychological components (Knapek & Kuritárné Szabó, 2014).

- Substance addiction within family dynamics, for example, as well as changes in how women's roles are seen in society, are examples of social components.

- Brain functioning is involved in biological factors, implying that the prefrontal cortex of a codependent person's brain falls short when it comes to controlling their empathic impulses. This is what makes them incapable of drawing that thin line, resulting in an excess of empathy and making it more difficult for them to say no.
- Psychological characteristics are typically associated with those who have suffered some form of abuse during childhood, such as domestic violence or neglect. As a result, they are more likely to be predisposed to care about others.

To summarize, codependency is not about caring or having feelings; both are appropriate and important, or else we would all be prone to narcissistic tendencies. Codependency implies that these activities and feelings are displayed and experienced in abnormal, excessive amounts, where responsibility for another takes precedence over responsibility for oneself and one's own needs.

We will look at some red flags that might help you determine whether you are in a codependent relationship as our next step.

Be Aware

Codependency symptoms include, to mention a few, compliance patterns, poor self-esteem patterns, denial patterns, and avoidance behaviors.

Let us take a deeper look at some of these patterns,

and if any of these resonate with you, it is time to take that first step toward making some real changes.

Avoidance Patterns

- You may find yourself avoiding any actions that may lead you to feel ashamed, rejected, or have wrath forced on you by the receiver.
- You have a high sense of judgment concerning the acts, ideas, and words of others.
- You have an underlying notion that emotional reactions are a sign of weakness.
- You tend to avoid any kind of disagreement and can be elusive or indirect.
- You avoid situations that make you feel vulnerable, such as physical, emotional, or sexual interaction.

Low Self-Esteem Patterns

- You are frequently unable to make a decision.
- You have a severe sense of self-judgment because you believe you are not good enough.
- You have difficulty recognizing yourself as a lovable person.
- Recognition, presents, and praise are all sources of discomfort.
- You value other people's feelings and views more than your own.
- You have difficulty expressing your requirements and needs.

Control Patterns

- You have a basic notion that individuals cannot appropriately care for themselves.

- Sex is utilized to gain favor and acceptance.
- When people reject offers of guidance or aid, it is common for bitterness and resentment to arise.
- You are overzealous in offering advice or information, even if it is not requested.
- You often shower gifts and favors on those you feel you need to persuade.
- You often use persuasion to encourage others to believe, feel, or act in a certain way.

Denial Patterns

- You often play down your own emotional experiences.
- You have trouble identifying the precise emotions you are experiencing.
- You consider yourself selfless and committed to the well-being of others.

Compliance Patterns

- You might think of sex as a replacement for love.
- You often allow your values, limits, and integrity to be jeopardized to avoid wrath and rejection from others.
- Others' wants and interests take precedence over your own.
- The ideas and sentiments of others are far more valuable than your own, and you are extremely sensitive to these emotions, even adopting them as your own at times.
- Fear prevents you from expressing your own, or distinct thoughts or emotions.

- You are overly faithful, even to the detriment of yourself.

In light of this, the best thing you can do for yourself is to contact a qualified counselor or therapist. You do not have to feel like you are walking on eggshells of any sort in any relationship.

And how does one go about addressing this problem? Let us have a look.

Cracking Codependency

The first step in breaking out of the vicious spiral that develops is to have a strong sense of self-awareness. Taking a proactive approach and seeking expert guidance is a surefire method to get this ball rolling and off to a terrific start.

Untangling these codependent behaviors will take time; nevertheless, having an awareness is the first seed sown. It will begin to sprout and grow a consciousness inside you that will help you understand that you genuinely deserve to live a happy, fulfilled life and that you have every right in the world to reclaim what is rightfully yours; your sense of self.

You might consider and use the following approaches as you proceed on your healing journey.

Patience Is a Virtue

You can gradually develop distance in the connection while you are making progress. Separating from someone, especially someone with whom you have a codependent relationship, is an extremely trying experience. Take your time and dedicate extra time to the tasks you wish to do as part of your path of self-discovery. Steer clear from any extreme decisions and behavior and remain focused on your healing.

Time to Stand Up

As you work on and improve your self-esteem, being able to stand up for yourself and what you believe in will become a lot easier. The capacity to maintain your ground and call someone out for activities that might negatively influence you, such as being undermined, criticized, or dominated, is crucial since it also communicates clear boundaries to the other person.

You Are Your Biggest Fan

Avoid the little voice in your head that has fallen into the trap of self-criticism. You will have to unlearn this, and the only way to do so is to catch those negative thoughts as they arise, hang on to them, examine them, recognize them for what they are; simply illogical assumptions, let them go and replace them with positive reinforcements. Keep an eye on your inner dialogue.

No Is Not Bad

Do not be scared to say "no" if you do not want to do anything for whatever reason. It is one of the strongest two-letter words available. In contrast to popular belief, the word "no" is a tool we may use to protect ourselves and communicate to others how far is too far regarding our personal space.

Direct Your Attention Inward

You will be astonished at how quickly you pick up on it after the initial learning curve. Focusing on oneself instead of others is an act of love toward yourself, not selfishness. If you do not take care of yourself first, you cannot take care of others in the first place.

Support

This will be mentioned multiple times throughout the book to emphasize the significance of having a solid support group. You might go beyond your close trusted acquaintances, such as family and friends, and find other like-minded people who are going through similar challenges as you by joining relevant support groups or networks. This can help you understand that you are not alone, as well as provide insight into your own situation from different viewpoints, or might bring something to your attention that was previously overlooked.

The first step toward recovery is understanding and recognizing the codependency indications, which is followed by self-awareness and proactive steps toward recovery. One thing to keep in mind during this whole process is to be kind and compassionate with yourself.

CHAPTER 5
POST-TRAUMATIC STRESS DISORDER

The conflict between the will to deny horrible events and the will to proclaim them aloud is the central dialectic of psychological trauma. —Judith Lewis

This is such a fitting quote for the first act of this chapter. Trauma is not restricted to the heroes who were summoned to the Vietnam War; it may be brought about by a variety of awful occurrences such as natural catastrophes, violence, rape, significant injury, and death, to mention a few.

Trauma is also not restricted to the individual who is directly affected by the heinous act; it may also be experienced secondhand, which refers to witnessing any of these events or living through these experiences. Any traumatic experience can lead to post-traumatic stress disorder, or PTSD, which can leave scars that are more agonizing than any physical scar from the same event.

This psychological condition has no prerequisites and nobody, irrespective of age, color, or culture, is immune to its vengeance.

What Is the Relationship?

It is well-established that traumatic experiences have a substantial influence on the brain, causing structural alterations and impeding normal brain function (American Psychiatric Association, 2019).

When we are stressed, the body goes into the notorious fight-or-flight response, which generates an avalanche of stress chemicals, such as cortisol, which directly influence the sections of your precious brain that play a role in your fear response, memory, decision-making capacity, and ability to think clearly. Unfortunately, the impact of stress on the regions that govern these responses has been demonstrated to dramatically reduce these functions (American Psychiatric Association, 2019).

The way abuse and trauma are related, in layman's terms, is due to the induction of a state of stress. The strategies used by abusers, including nonviolent ones, to establish authority and control over their victims leave the victims in a continual state of stress. Threats, punishment, and verbal abuse are just a few types of abusive conduct that can result in trauma symptoms. Simply put, abusive relationships are traumatic in and of themselves.

Symptoms of PTSD

When it comes to detecting PTSD symptoms, they can start popping up within a month of having a traumatic experience, yet symptoms may not even appear until years later.

These symptoms are, in most circumstances, as severe as the incident itself, wreaking havoc in the lives of its victims and making regular living appear like a distant, unattainable recollection from the past that is overshadowed and continually plagued by trauma. Mood, thinking patterns, emotional responses, and physical reactions all change.

PTSD symptoms are classified into four categories:

Avoidance

This happens when a person steers clear of circumstances, people, places, or events that can trigger memories of the traumatic event or anything connected to it. This avoidance tendency could extend to recalling, discussing, or considering the specific circumstance; concealing it in mental depths almost as if it never occurred.

Alterations in Cognition and Mood

In brief, PTSD causes significant cognitive and emotional alterations in its victims, resulting in an emotional and mental hot mess. The following could occur:

- Distorted thoughts about oneself and others,

brought about by severe negative thoughts and emotions.

- Feelings of detachment.
- Loss of interest in activities that used to provide a great deal of joy and pleasure.
- A distorted recollection of the event, whether it is the cause or the repercussions. This might take the form of self-blame, guilt, rage, humiliation, dread, or terror.
- An inability to experience positive emotions.

Alterations in Arousal and Reactivity

This is frequently a protective strategy that is unconsciously adopted to prevent any more stress, some of these behaviors might include:

- Exhibiting irresponsible or reckless conduct.
- Feeling tense and easily startled.
- Showing regular outbreaks of rage.
- Exhibiting problems with maintaining a good sleeping routine.
- Experiencing concentration and attention issues.
- Feeling irritated and unduly distrustful of others or one's surroundings.

Intrusion

This often alludes to an assault of uncontrollable, intrusive thoughts which might include the following:

- Having recurring nightmares or disturbing dreams.
- Experiencing recurring flashbacks.

- Reliving the painful incident regularly through the recollection of memories.

As you can notice, these symptoms are not something that one can just stick a bandaid over or use a home remedy on. These symptoms are also not one size fits all, the intensity of symptoms varies over time, which could be exacerbated during stressful periods, or reminders that serve as triggers to unleash the emotions of the past.

PTSD and Recovery

It is strongly advised that those suffering from PTSD get professional treatment from psychiatrists or therapists who specialize in treating individuals suffering from PTSD; there are no shortcuts around this.

When it comes to treating PTSD, different strategies have been used with great outcomes. PTSD is commonly accompanied by depression, panic disorder, recurrent trauma, and drug misuse, so learning to live with it is well worth a try in terms of obtaining good therapy, as it may help re-establish a sense of safety and equip you with stronger coping abilities.

In all honesty, deciding to reach out and seek help is difficult, but once done, the silver lining emerges. Treatment may entail counseling or medication of a particular kind; depending on the specific circumstances, both may be necessary.

Talk therapy such as cognitive behavioral therapy (CBT) is one of the therapies utilized in dealing with and recovering from PTSD by helping sufferers better understand and recognize symptoms, triggers, and coping skills to better manage their PTSD. Cognitive processing therapy, which helps to reframe negative thoughts and experiences, and prolonged exposure therapy, which enables victims to face fears and negative emotions by incorporating gradual exposure to things that they have avoided since the occurrence of trauma, are two types of CBT therapy that stand out in the management of PTSD.

It is reasonable to conclude that emotional abuse causes trauma, which has serious negative repercussions. As a result, it is critical to withdraw yourself immediately from any circumstance where you are facing any sort of emotional abuse.

PTSD is a significant mental health condition that affects and erodes your thoughts, emotions, and memories, causing you to live in a permanent state of terror, confusion, and at times delusion.

CHAPTER 6
BREAKING FREE FROM UNHEALTHY PATTERNS

W hy do we, as humans, become stuck on some things in life and resort to avoidance tactics, at best attempting every tiny shortcut along the way?

Is it due to fear? Perhaps. We dread the unknown because it is frightening to move outside of our comfort zone. The worst thing is that many of us will remain in relationships that are incredibly harmful to us because of this fear; in abusive settings, this dread is most often imposed onto a person by depriving them of their self-esteem and self-identity, leaving them as empty as a void, left to ponder how they could possibly survive beyond the known, as brutally destructive as it is.

This abusive circumstance then becomes the new "normal" because the way you respond to your uncomfortable feelings and experiences begins to develop patterns in your life. You may believe that by acting in particular ways, such as not asking too many questions or not seeing your friends and family as frequently as you used to, you are fixing some difficulties. These are not solutions, but perhaps you believe they are because you believe they will maintain peace in the given relationship; however, they actually create new problems or exacerbate existing ones.

In the late 1960s, Stephen Karpman proposed a wonderful model that depicts conflict and drama in intensive interpersonal connections, which is commonly referred to as destructive social interaction (Davies, 2019). It is called the Karpman Drama Triangle, and I would love to share this insight with you to give you a better understanding of the dynamics of an abusive relationship.

The Karpman Drama Triangle

This drama triangle effectively captures the narcissist dynamic as well as other types of toxic relationships.

Let me start with the basics: the triangle is made up of three separate roles: victim, persecutor, and rescuer. These are only the roles represented; in certain cases, there may be two, three, or even more individuals engaged, who take on these different roles. These roles are interchangeable, so anyone in the specific dynamic can switch between them at any moment, allowing the dynamic to fluctuate and evolve continually. Even if some parties do not knowingly expose others to manipulation, it is unavoidable since manipulation, whether consciously or unconsciously, is a component of this dysfunctional connection. In other words, whether or not everyone involved is aware of it, manipulation is the game, and everyone involved is playing it.

Let us have a closer look at these characters.

The Victim

Even if you are a victim of abuse, keep in mind that the victim role in this dynamic does not reflect on you as a person or your position in suffering abuse in the relationship; rather, it portrays the roles that all parties in the relationship and its exchanges can possibly take on. For instance, when it comes to this relationship, the abuser might sometimes switch roles and play the victim as well. Narcissists, in particular, make effective use of the victim role to avoid and escape accountability, of any kind. This is ideal in a narcissistic environment since it allows the person to deflect responsibility and be "rescued" at the same time.

Depending on the person and scenario, the victim takes a position of pain and injustice, along with feelings of resentment, persecution, oppression, fear, or humiliation. The issue with being the victim in this sort of relationship is often not the abuse, but rather adopting a victim mindset.

Unfortunately, being a victim in an abusive relationship makes you so accustomed to the characteristics of this role that they become habitual, your new distorted state of "normal", so that even if the abuser is no longer present, another will be sought to replace that abuser for you to continue experiencing that "familiar" state of suffering.

What is the aim of all of this?

To be consoled and receive sympathy.

The Persecutor

This position, especially when carried on by the abuser, represents them in their full-fledged element; analogous to them seizing their throne. This attitude is characterized by oppressive conduct, blame, control, shame, arrogance, and authoritative, intimidating traits.

This domineering stance typically diminishes the worth of others by inflicting shame and guilt on the victims or recipients of their fury. This includes classic narcissistic, abusive thinking processes like "I am right and you are wrong", and the master-servant dynamic.

What is their main game?

Shifting blame and avoiding responsibility.

The Rescuer

This individual believes that saving others is their calling. This is done not because they are Mother Teresa, but rather to raise their self-esteem as opposed to providing genuine assistance.

Another factor that makes this position appear less

sincere is that it actually plays a significant role in perpetuating the poisonous dynamic of the given relationship. Responding to the victim's helplessness, whether real or feigned, the rescuer reasserts responsibility on the victim's behalf; in fact, they tend to be unduly responsible for their own poor self-esteem. This is the quintessential enabling, codependent, people-pleasing persona.

Sometimes the rescuer will step into this position without being asked, taking on tasks that pertain to someone else. Narcissists readily switch to this position as a coping mechanism for emotions of guilt, worry, or dread.

What do they gain from all of this?

Simply boosting their own self-worth.

This is a narcissist's ideal playground, changing shape and moving between these roles, victim, persecutor, and savior, playing it all like a game of chess to gain control over another person.

Scenario

The majority of abusive relationships begin when the abuser comes to the aid of the other person who is experiencing difficulties. They, like predators, detect a time of vulnerability and strike to develop some type of reliance.

You are caught and knee-deep in it, and the game begins with the narcissist assuming a part and assigning positions in the dynamic, drawing people in. As a result, unhealthy relationship patterns such as drama, dependence, and conflict are generated. With time, these roles shift, further forging the dysfunctional relationship, which is fueled by poisonous attributes.

Let us take a look at a real-life example.

In a relationship, one spouse is abusive, playing the persecutor role, while the other partner is on the receiving end of this abuse, playing the victim.

The spouse who has taken on the victim character is exhausted by the constant abuse and chooses to seek help from a friend. In response, the friend responds by playing the position of the rescuer, desiring to step in and save their buddy by convincing them to quit the toxic relationship. As a result, he becomes a type of hero, a rescuer. This, however, backfires.

The buddy, the rescuer, motivates the victim to confront the abuser, but this is met with surprise when the abuser adopts the role of the victim. In their new victim role, the abuser begs and offers forgiveness to the previous victim. This might include expressing something to the effect that they cannot live without the other person and that they messed up because they are truly wounded and require support.

And just like that, the original victim steps right back into the poisonous relationship to save the wolf in sheep's clothing, the abuser appearing as the victim.

What about the initial rescuer, the friend?

As any friend, they would wonder why the initial victim is returning to the destructively abusive relationship. This prompts the initial victim to take on the role of the persecutor, becoming defensive and disputing their friend's judgments. Now the friend that was the original rescuer takes on a new role, that of the victim.

As you can see, the individual who is the victim in an abusive relationship transitioned from victim to rescuer to persecutor, inevitably resuming the position of the victim again. And there you have it, the abusive cycle.

The abuser transitioned from persecutor to victim, which is characteristic of narcissistic traits. The involved buddy changed from being the rescuer to the victim. This is clearly not a healthy dynamic, since it creates vicious spirals with bad tendencies.

How do you get out of this?

Breaking the Pattern

One of the most crucial components of changing old habits and creating new ones is developing a sense of self-awareness. This is significant since it reveals your level of engagement and the impact you have on your current circumstance.

This information, in turn, will help you better grasp how to stop contributing to the pattern and, ultimately, break free from it.

The Victim

To be able to disrupt the victim pattern in situations like these, it is critical to understand that actions speak louder than words in this context. Talking about the unfavorable circumstance and its consequences will not solve the problem; but, taking physical action by employing necessary intervention techniques would.

You cannot change other people; you can only change yourself, and you must speak out for yourself. Relying solely on external action to come to your aid would be wishful thinking. It is also critical to recognize that you have choices. Everything you do is a choice, and understanding this is how you may reclaim your power and control in situations like these. Nobody has the authority to make decisions for you but yourself.

Guilt-tripping and feeling ashamed are unavoidable for victims, but the most powerful tool you will have is realizing that you do not have to justify yourself and that you are not there to meet the needs of others. Everyone is accountable for their own happiness.

The Persecutor

For victims who find themselves moving into this position, breaking away from the persecutor role is essential. In all honesty, utilizing these methods and seeing positive results is improbable for narcissists and abusers alike.

I am not saying people cannot change; they can, as previously said. Nevertheless, some kind of therapy intervention would be required as with these personality types, admittance, empathy, and true regret fall far short.

However, if you find yourself in this situation, the greatest thing you can do is cease criticizing or questioning people. Recognize that everyone has the right to their viewpoint, and remember that you have options. You are the only one who has complete control over your life. Being a victim of abuse means giving up control, which is precisely what you need to reclaim, thus losing control over your emotions is merely another way of losing your power. Navigate difficult circumstances without confrontation, anger, or hostility.

It is critical to look within and focus on yourself since negative behavior toward others and the drive to control are a mirror of one's own deep-seated anxieties.

The Rescuer

The traditional people-pleasing notion of the rescue role is symptomatic of, once again, low self-esteem.

This persistent low self-esteem ghost is silenced by intervening and striving to resolve and help others. This is not the way to tackle the problem; instead, aim to help others without expecting anything in return. Do it out of the goodness of your heart, without expecting any benefit in the form of increased self-esteem, in other words, a personal boost of your sense of self.

Is your assistance genuinely required, and is it sought?

Allow things to run their course rather than thrusting yourself into situations, especially if you are not asked to help in any way. Help can only be given to those who truly want to be helped and those who ask for it. The most essential thing to remember is that helping and supporting others should not come at the price of your own happiness and well-being.

The more you understand the indicators of each position in abusive dynamics, the easier it is to notice when and how they play out, giving you a greater chance of resisting getting dragged into these patterns.

When one member leaves the triangle, the pattern ceases to exist, and mistreatment against the victim in an abusive relationship ceases, at least until the abuser can find someone else to replace that role.

Let us take it a step further and look at how you may prioritize yourself and set proper boundaries.

CHAPTER 7
PRIORITIZE YOURSELF AND SET BOUNDARIES

❧

Prioritizing oneself implies putting yourself first; it is a skill well worth developing.

This may be easier said than done, especially for victims of abuse since they are utterly pressured into abandoning power, thus losing their sense of self which makes it much more difficult to reclaim and maintain a healthy regard for themselves.

Engaging in self-care, creating appropriate, safe boundaries, and practicing self-compassion are the foundations of a fulfilled life. Prioritizing yourself is not selfish; it helps you to care for yourself, which allows you to care for others; similarly, boundaries are not selfish; they are intended to safeguard you and preserve your sense of self.

After all, how can you enjoy life if you are not doing the things that you like and that make you happy? It is about more than simply making you joyful; it is also about self-discovery. Unfortunately, this is an additional component that is severely hampered in abusive relationships since you are a captive, only functioning to satisfy the purpose and demands of an abusive person.

So, what is the significance of prioritizing yourself?

An Unselfish Art

To answer the preceding question, consider why it is critical to prioritize yourself in your own life. Actually, if you repeat that sentence, it is quite reasonable to think that the only person who should come first in your life is you, simply because no one else has the right or privilege to live your life, it is a gift that is tailor-made and only intended for you.

If Your Cup Is Empty

How can you give if you do not have anything to give? Charity starts at home, and in this sense, it means that being compassionate and understanding towards yourself allows you to be more supportive and understanding toward others.

Life is already full of demands that must be met outside of ourselves, so making time to prioritize yourself and step away from the rat race is essential for staying grounded. However, being in any type of abusive relationship drastically changes the game, and prioritizing yourself becomes non-existent.

One of the best things you can do to take back your power is to set aside time for yourself to practice self-care and self-reflection. When you do things for others and it comes from a place where you truly have something to offer rather than a place where you feel you merely have to meet the requirements, you will notice a profound difference. Because it shifts your attitude toward yourself, self-care allows you to shift your attitude toward your responsibilities and toward others.

Your Inner Critic

Oh, that all-too-familiar little inner critic that we all have hanging around inside our heads. It can be helpful at times, but it can also be your worst enemy.

This inner critic is amplified in abusive environments, convincing you that you must achieve certain goals to feel a sense of worth, belonging, and acceptance. The most important thing to keep in mind when doing anything is why you are doing it in the first place. Are you doing it because you genuinely want to help or be productive? Are you doing it to fulfill other deep-seated desires? Are you doing it to meet the needs and requirements of others? Do you prioritize the needs of others over your own?

Be wary of your inner critic, as it can also reinforce the ideals imposed on you by an abuser, leading you to believe that anything you do for yourself is completely selfish. The main issue with this is that it not only affects your mood and behavior, but it also fosters an unrealistic desire to constantly please others, as well as a need for perfection.

This sends you into an unrealistic spiral in which you lose track of not only yourself, but also reality, and end up living a life half-lived.

Self-Compassion Suffers

When life consists primarily of tending to the needs of others, self-compassion tends to suffer. How is this even possible?

Simply put, your awareness is primarily tied to others, thus you will be unable to be mindful of your own needs and feelings. Self-compassion not only allows you to recognize who you are and what you need, but it also allows you to better recognize your mistakes and shortcomings, allowing you to make changes to improve and grow as a person.

When you have a deeper understanding of yourself, you will have the magical ability to not be overly judgmental of yourself; you will better understand your self-worth and feel more comfortable with yourself, thus, being better able to extend the same understanding and acceptance to others.

Losing Yourself

Whether it is through our work or attending to the needs of others, we have a propensity to blur the lines between doing things to prove our worth and doing things because they are worthwhile for us. This is particularly true in all abusive relationships.

This raises the risk of losing sight of our actual interests and purpose, which makes it challenging to connect with oneself. In essence, you are sacrificing parts of yourself while ignoring the things that truly fulfill and make you happy.

These are just a few examples of the consequences that can occur when you fail to prioritize yourself. Let us look at a few approaches you can take to begin mastering the art of prioritizing yourself.

All About Prioritizing

As admirable as it is to be there for others, it is even better to be there for yourself by prioritizing your needs; otherwise, you risk losing sight of who you are as a person. A terribly hefty price to pay in my opinion.

Let us have a look at some simple approaches you can take in order to avoid this terrible fate from knocking at your door.

Slow Down

Oh, the rat race, the delicate act of balancing our lives, and our inclination to constantly want to appear in control.

You lose sight of the enjoyment that comes from partaking in activities because you are constantly rushing from one obligation to the next to check items off the list. Slow down and smell the roses. When you deliberately minimize the pressure, you will start to enjoy things more as you experience less anxiety and stress. Even if you only have ten minutes to spare, you could practice mindfulness and check in with yourself during this time for instance.

Being Number One

Putting yourself first means that you must, at times, literally put yourself first. Rather than chasing after everyone else first thing in the morning, invest in yourself. Practice yoga, meditate, or read something inspiring. You must be proactive in making time for yourself in your schedule. A schedule does not exist for you to run around most of your time and people-please.

Self-Discovery

Maybe you are a parent, a partner, or a business executive. But what if you were stripped of all your titles, identities, and roles that you play on a daily basis?

Will you recognize yourself? Will you remain the same person in essence? To take on the task of self-discovery, know your values, and better comprehend your true identity, it is imperative to regularly engage in self-reflection. One of the finest ways to take care of yourself and live your best life is by getting right to the heart of who you really are.

Self-Talk

Yes, your inner voice comes into play again, and with good reason. It has a significant impact not only on your mood and thoughts but also on your self-perception. Thus, be aware of the things you say to yourself.

How do you talk to yourself? Gently as you would with a friend or dismissive perhaps? Be kinder when talking to yourself, even if you feel disheartened, you need compassion. Replace negative words and thoughts with more positive reinforcements instead.

You could, for example, repeat the following positive mantras:

- I am important
- I deserve to be happy
- I have got this
- I am giving it my best

Exclaim Your Worth

Mirror mirror on the wall. Oh yes, you are going to have to employ this strategy. Make it a daily practice to look into the mirror and tell yourself that you are enough, you are indeed perfectly adequate. This might feel a bit awkward at first; however, this message will start sinking in with enough repetition and before it is a day too late or a dollar too short, you will start believing it. Do not stand there and judge your imperfections, you are standing there to focus on, and highlight your strengths.

Making yourself a priority enables you to be your happiest self—not just for yourself, but also for those around you. You are your most valuable asset and not someone else's, that is merely a romantic notion; thus, investing in yourself every day and ensuring your values and emotions are aligned with your actions will only yield the greatest returns.

When it comes to prioritizing yourself, there is one more thing that should not be overlooked: setting proper boundaries. Let us get started.

Bouncing Back With Boundaries

Again, this is not selfish; rather, it is critical in showing others what is and is not acceptable when it comes to us as individuals.

Setting boundaries is not done to offend others; in fact, it is done to keep you safe and to protect your values and beliefs. These boundaries are frequently shifted or ignored in abusive relationships, but in reality, they should never be tampered with or compromised.

Easier said than done right? Indeed, it is fairly common to prioritize the needs of others over our own, especially when it comes to loved ones. Setting boundaries is yet another tool for prioritizing yourself, another method of self-care. And you are well aware that in order to provide and care for others, you must ensure that your cup is not only full, but overflowing.

Boundaries vary depending on who we are as people and our circumstances. You may be more strict with your boundaries at work compared to when you are at home for instance. But, regardless of how flexible you are or what type of boundaries are put in place, one thing is certain: Proper, healthy boundaries are important.

Here are a few guidelines for what healthy boundaries might look like:

- accepting "no" as an answer
- knowing how to properly communicate your wants and needs
- placing value on your own opinions
- refraining from oversharing information, especially personal information

It is all about you, so let us take a look at why setting proper boundaries is important when it comes to protecting yourself as a person.

Maintain Healthy Relationships

Healthy boundaries equal healthy relationships because they maintain the delicate balance between interdependence and independence.

Stating what you are and are not okay with will almost certainly result in more peaceful, fulfilling interactions. You will be able to avoid feelings of resentment because by drawing a line that helps others better understand what is not only expected but also required when it comes to your needs in any successful interaction, you will be able to keep your peace.

You Are Not Pushed Over

Of course, we must compromise in life; however, compromising does not imply that you should be unhappy, violated, or ignored.

Compromise occurs when a level playing field is established between two people and both are satisfied to some extent with the given outcome. When you compromise, you must still be assertive and able to express your feelings and needs; this will keep you from ending up in situations in which you do not want to be or belong.

The need for assertiveness arises when setting boundaries. This means defending your rights and interests, even if they conflict with those of the other party. In short, you must learn to use the word "no" effectively.

Prevent Burnout

Burnout, which is defined as any kind of mental or physical exhaustion, has been shown to negatively impact our mental health and make us much more prone to depression and anxiety (Koutsimani et al., 2019).

Now, what does the concept of boundaries have to do with burnout?

When your boundaries are crossed, the needs of others are placed above your own to your own disadvantage and you are ultimately sacrificing yourself.

This might occur in all spheres of life—bringing work home, accepting obligations that are not yours, or giving up any semblance of freedom. You are not only dispersing your precious time too thinly, but you also end up feeling blue, having trouble focusing, and failing to fulfill your obligations.

Let us examine a few distinct boundaries and how they might be stated in an assertive yet non-aggressive manner.

Setting Proper Boundaries

Because our lives are filled with so many different aspects, various boundaries exist to accompany these.

Where does one begin when it comes to establishing firm boundaries?

By considering the various types of personal boundaries for a better understanding.

- Physical boundaries include anything physically related to you, such as privacy, personal space, and your body. For example, if you are a hugger when greeting others, you may discover that some people do not appreciate this form of contact.
- Your beliefs, thoughts, and ideas are all part of your intellectual boundaries. When any of these aspects of a person is dismissed or ignored, these boundaries are crossed. Insulting someone because of their different points of view is a common example of crossing an intellectual boundary.
- Emotional boundaries, as the name implies, are all about emotions and how comfortable you

are sharing them with a particular person. Perhaps you do not want to share every emotion you are experiencing with a friend, or perhaps it takes you longer to open up to others about your feelings.

- In terms of intimacy, sexual boundaries are what you allow and are comfortable with. This could include sexual actions, remarks, or other preferences.
- Financial boundaries are all about money and the way you manage it. This could include things like being a spender or preferring to save your money.

It is critical to clear any ambiguities about your boundaries to identify and maintain a healthy sense of self by limiting your exposure to stressors and reinforcing your mental health.

The following are excellent approaches to stepping into yourself and avoiding emotionally draining burdens.

Baby Steps

Because you can easily become overwhelmed, the best thing you can do is to start slowly and implement one boundary at a time.

Do not try to impose a slew of rules right away. Again, it is not a race, but rather a process by which the perfect fit is attained. If you want to know whether your boundaries are fulfilling your needs or not, you will need to go through reflection periods.

Consistency Is Key

Consistency is important in most aspects of life, and it is especially important when it comes to boundaries since it prevents ambiguity and makes the lines distinct for both you and other people.

Your consistency will also help to reinforce and uphold your boundaries, making them a permanent aspect of your life.

You Are Your Own Reinforcement

Boundaries are difficult to establish, and this is especially true if you are in or breaking free from an abusive relationship.

All of the negativity that you are constantly exposed to is not exactly conducive to a healthy mindset. However, you can strike back by changing your internal dialogue, your inner voice. Reinforce your mental well-being, value, and self-worth by practicing self-compassion and feeding your mind messages that you are deserving—because you are.

Self-Reflection

When it comes to boundaries, self-reflection is essential; it serves as a springboard from which you can set out and determine how far is too far.

We frequently experience things without questioning why they elicit certain emotions in us. It is critical to pause and reflect on events in your life. What caused you to react the way you did when a specific event occurred? Investigate your emotions and determine the source of their existence to help you better understand how to set proper healthy boundaries.

Clear Communication

You must communicate your boundaries clearly. Being assertive is necessary, but it is important to remember that being assertive does not imply being confrontational.

When your boundaries are crossed, stand up for your beliefs and express your concerns. This could be extremely difficult for someone who has been abused. As previously stated, you could make your point calmly and assertively, and if the situation escalates, simply leave because your boundaries are non-negotiable, and standing up for your values is more than just making a point; it is a way of protecting yourself.

Adapt

Although they cannot be negotiated, boundaries are something that can be strengthened and built upon.

Your boundaries will need to alter and adapt as you develop as a person, so it is critical to reflect in order to make the necessary adjustments, keep your boundaries current, and ensure that they work for you.

Respect Others Boundaries

Setting your own boundaries is important, but so is understanding and respecting the boundaries of others.

It does not have to be a huge mystery or a guessing game. If you are unsure about something concerning another person's boundaries, simply ask. Ask when it would be best to get in touch with someone instead of just contacting them directly; rather than assuming that someone would enjoy watching the same series as you, inquire as to what they would prefer to watch. These are just a few examples, but asking rather than assuming or imposing is a far more considerate and thoughtful approach.

By now you undoubtedly understand what boundaries are and you can add that you understand how to begin implementing them. Mastering this skill is life-changing, a profoundly powerful way of freeing yourself from stress, resentment, and disappointment.

Let us keep navigating the storm toward brighter days by taking a closer look at obsessive thinking next.

CHAPTER 8
OBSESSIVE THINKING AND OCD

W̶e all worry, and healthy worry usually results in a solution or acceptance. Then there is the dark side of worry; obsessive thinking, which is clouded with obsession, worry, and rumination with no end in sight or ability to seize control of the distressing thoughts and images that replay in your mind like a broken record.

Obsessive thinking is a major indicator of obsessive compulsive disorder, or OCD, and other types of anxiety disorders in which you become a hostage to your runaway thoughts, exacerbating your anxiety and leaving you vulnerable to an onslaught of obsessions (Kelly, 2020). Being continuously hyper-focused on negative thoughts reinforces unhealthy routines and detrimental emotional states, leaving you lost in a sea of despair, bewilderment, and anger. If this torturous cycle of thoughts goes unchecked you can find yourself further sinking into the depths of depression and other damaging behaviors.

But how does emotional abuse expose you to this type of torture?

It is no secret that emotional abuse causes significant psychological damage that haunts victims long after the relationship ends, impairing their perception of themselves and the world around them (Kelly, 2020). The purposefully imposed bewilderment, shame, self-loathing, and guilt creates tremendous amounts of confusion, which causes repetitive, destructive thought patterns that may even be inescapable for the likes of Houdini.

However, transforming from a victim to a survivor and reclaiming your life does not necessitate any magic or trickery; it simply necessitates unlocking your inherent inner strength through educating yourself about all aspects of emotional abuse.

Let us confront obsessive thinking head-on.

What Is the Connection?

Obsessive thinking is a symptom of OCD, which is extremely intrusive and can result in repetitive compulsive behaviors (Kelly, 2020).

We can compare these experiences to an image in which the mind is a ship without a captain, in complete lack of control amidst a mental storm that is bringing gushes of stress and anxiety.

The errors in thinking caused by OCD are known as cognitive distortions; these distortions are the keys that unlock various obsessions and compulsions, such as obsessive thinking, which skews the person's perception of pretty much everything, including themselves, as previously stated (Kelly, 2020). As a result, it is no surprise that these distortions are associated with mood and anxiety disorders like post-traumatic stress disorder, panic disorder, and general anxiety disorder, to name a few. Again, you can see that these disorders are all unfortunately linked to the consequences of emotional abuse.

Thus, it is critical to recognize that when you find yourself overthinking, it may not be a simple case of a racing mind; pay close attention because if it is accompanied by feelings of anxiety and distress, and seems completely inescapable, you are most likely an obsessive thinker.

Let us take a look at what cognitive distortions are and how to recognize them.

Placing Over-Importance on Thoughts

It is not uncommon for people suffering from OCD and obsessive thinking to have dark thoughts that are beyond comprehension, thoughts that they would never consider saying to another person.

Consider the possibility of physically harming someone. When it comes to cognitive distortions, the issue is that thoughts and actions can be confused. The person may mistakenly believe that if they are thinking these thoughts, they truly believe they are capable of such things. Thus, the meaning attached to these thoughts can cause doubt and isolation, as well as ostracization from others, regardless of whether these thoughts are put into action or not.

Over-Inflation of Responsibility

This is essentially a situation in which the person may have an over-inflated sense of responsibility for certain things.

This can lead to distorted thinking in which they believe that if a specific responsibility is not met, there will be catastrophic, life-threatening consequences. They believe it is the end of the world. Perhaps if they do not prepare the required breakfast, the rest of the person they are preparing it for's day will be terrible and they may lose their job.

Yes, this may seem far-fetched, but these are the distorted realities that one could experience.

Needing Certainty

It is very common to feel the need for reassurance, even when doing so is unrealistic at times, and is typically done to help reduce anxiety.

Sadly, when it comes to cognitive distortions this persistent desire for certainty is also a form of avoidance behavior, and all it accomplishes is reinforcing these anxious notions and keeping one in an unavoidable state of tension.

Overestimating Danger

With cognitive distortions, the likelihood of danger is grossly overestimated, and the consequences are completely and unrealistically blown out of proportion, further fueling compulsions.

Someone experiencing this may have recurring thoughts that their relationship is likely to end and that if they put one foot wrong, it is the end. This may cause them to overcompensate in their behavior, which is exacerbated in abusive relationships by the abuser.

Intolerance of Emotional Discomfort

It is frightening to experience intense negative emotions, especially when they are accompanied by distorted beliefs that experiencing them will result in negative consequences such as having a psychological breakdown, being overwhelmed, and losing everything.

Thus, constant reassurance and avoidance behaviors are synonymous with cognitive distortions in attempts to avoid any negative emotional experiences.

As you can see, these mental experiences can make anyone feel as if they are trapped in a living nightmare, and unfortunately, in abusive relationships, this is not met with empathy and understanding, but rather viewed as a weakness that should be exploited for control and personal gain.

These thoughts that cause fear and amplify anxiety

cause such terrible distress that the person experiencing them will do anything to get rid of them, and hence the floodgates open to compulsive behaviors in an attempt to silence these intrusions. This mental trap is brought forth by the alterations in brain chemistry that are brought forth by anxiety, which makes it extremely challenging to shift perspective and see the positive aspects in life. Thus, it is very important to remember that if you are experiencing these thoughts, it is not your fault, and it is not easy to silence them or distract yourself.

Making it Stop

If I told you to stop thinking about the big pink elephant in the room, I am guessing the chances of you succeeding are slim.

This is not an assumption; studies have shown that the more you want to avoid thinking about something, the more likely you are to think about it (Wegner et al., 1987). This futile strategy is because by making an effort to forget something, your brain is reminded that it still exists.

This is exacerbated for those who have obsessive thoughts because, when combined with fear and shame, getting rid of intrusive thoughts is extremely difficult. The good news is that it is not impossible.

Addressing the underlying cause of the issue, which is anxiety, is the key to more effectively managing obsessive thinking.

Let us take a look at some steps you can take to get started if you struggle with obsessive thinking.

Acceptance

Accepting your thoughts for what they are may seem brave to say, but it is vital. They do not define you; we all have little control over the thoughts that run through our heads on a daily basis, whether we have anxiety or OCD or not; this is normal.

What counts is how you respond to those thoughts; some can be accepted and embraced, while others must be let go of. Try not to resist these obsessive thoughts if you observe yourself experiencing them; just let them be since they will pass subsequently. They lose their influence on you if you accept them. Recognize them, do not fight or hide them; in fact, do not be afraid or ashamed of them.

Spend time with them and question them to gain a better understanding; you will realize that they are not there to control you; rather, you are the true master. Nothing in this world has meaning aside from the meaning we give it.

Journaling

Keeping a journal of these intrusive, obsessive thoughts can help you understand them better.

You can evaluate their occurrence to see if there are any underlying patterns or triggers, such as specific times, places, or things. This also allows you to pull them from the depths of your mind and process them in a new way. Seeing them as words will also remind you that your thoughts are not there to control you.

Cognitive Behavioral Therapy

Cognitive behavioral therapy, or CBT, is a type of therapy that has proven to be very effective in treating a variety of mental disorders, including obsessive thoughts (Dibdin, 2022).

This type of therapy focuses on changing automatic negative thoughts that negatively impact your life by providing actionable solutions that will change the way you think and behave.

Ground Yourself

These thoughts either pull you back into the past or catapult you into the future; in any case, it is not a holiday to be plagued by worries about the past or the future. What is truly important is the present.

Thus, focusing on the present moment keeps you grounded; after all, the present moment is the only time when we have true power to change things for the better. You can practice being present by engaging in mindfulness, meditation, or deep breathing exercises, for example.

A Magical Mantra

When these thoughts arise, recall, memorize, and repeat these words: This will also pass.

Every thought will pass, even though some have a

tendency to linger longer than others. There is no such thing as a permanent state of mind. A technique you may use to help you refocus on the here and now and lessen the power that thoughts have over you, is to have a simple mantra ready to chant as those intrusive thoughts pop up.

Be Curious

This is, in my opinion, a highly inventive approach. Be curious about these thoughts rather than being intimidated and ashamed by them.

Your brain will interpret your thoughts differently if you reframe them by viewing them objectively and adopting a more curious attitude. Observe how your body reacts to the thoughts and pay attention to the emotions elicited in you.

Thought Clouds

A mindfulness exercise called "thought clouds" asks you to picture a clear blue sky in your head and your thoughts as clouds (Dibdin, 2022).

As in nature, there are different kinds of clouds; some are ominous and gloomy while others are fluffy and white. However, none of them are long-lasting. Eventually, they all drift away to expose the brilliant blue sky. This will help you perceive these thoughts from a different angle and prevent them from overwhelming you.

It is critical to remember that not all obsessive

thoughts are symptoms of anxiety or OCD. If these thoughts do not occur frequently or have a significant negative impact on your life, it is unlikely that you have OCD. If these haunting thoughts cause you constant distress, it is highly advised that you seek professional help and speak with a licensed therapist.

CHAPTER 9
ABANDONMENT FEARS

For abusers, using weaknesses as weapons is what it is all about, so threats of abandonment are typically a standard weapon used to instill fear when it comes to emotional manipulation.

Nobody handles abandonment well; it is a painful experience for most people, depending on the circumstances. However, abandonment should not be viewed solely in terms of leaving an empty hole in the soul. Let us take a step back and look at it from a different perspective: Abandonment in an emotionally abusive relationship.

Abandonment has unique interpretations in emotionally abusive relationships because it is not a one-time event with a grand finale in which the abuser rides off into the sunset. Oh no, you are abandoned over and over in various ways, emotionally toyed with. Here are some classic examples of how abusers use this nasty trick:

- Perhaps you walked out during one of your

first arguments.

- Siding with others in a given situation, rather than offering you support.
- Ridiculing you or decimating something you genuinely enjoy and care about.
- Making negative remarks about your relationship.
- Declaring what a terrible partner or spouse you are.

Does any of this resonate?

Let us continue and take an in-depth look at abandonment, how to recognize it, and the steps you can take with regard to healing from it.

What Are the Characteristics?

Abandonment issues are frequently linked to childhood trauma when there has been a traumatic loss, such as abandonment, death, or rejection.

It is not, however, limited to childhood trauma; we are all susceptible to experiencing and developing abandonment issues at any point in our lives as a result of being exposed to neglect or abuse in some form or another. In terms of relationships, any trauma, such as abuse, a cheating partner, or divorce, are all examples of triggers that can lead to abandonment issues.

Let us get another topic off the table here, one that has a lot to do with abandonment issues: attachment styles. Attachment style, as the name implies, refers to how you connect with those around you. The attachment style you develop is critical because it greatly influences and determines the future of the given relationship (Smith, 2022).

Attachment Styles

The unfortunate reality of being exposed to some form of trauma or abuse during a relationship can lead to the development of unhealthy attachment styles, which we will discuss next.

Anxious Attachment

This attachment style is distinguished by an excessive desire to be loved, accepted, and feel close to a specific person.

This desire is often extreme, and the person will experience feelings of not being worthy of love or attention, constantly overcompensating to ensure that their ultimate fear, abandonment, does not become a reality. The negative aspects are condensed to insecurity, anxiety, and low self-worth.

Avoidant Attachment

This attachment style is all about having difficulty forming close, intimate connections because independence is deemed to be preferable to the possibility of being hurt.

Intimacy in any form is a true struggle, and it is generally avoided as much as possible as a means of self-preservation and protection. A person may be mistakenly labeled as mean or cold, but they are not;

they simply have difficulty opening up to others and exposing that level of vulnerability.

Disorganized Attachment

Here, the attachment style is formed when a person is exposed to competing behaviors, such as a partner who never leaves your side but with whom you hardly ever engage.

Perhaps they are sweet one minute and dismissive the next, as is the typical hot-and-cold scenario. This causes a great deal of confusion for the person on the receiving end of the stick, leading to conflict and anxiety because there is uncertainty about whether or not one is truly loved.

Secure Attachment

Secure attachment is a healthy attachment style characterized by warmth, openness, and self-content. This approach emerges when a person is respected, cherished, and given encouragement. And certainly, it has all the positive traits of a good relationship, such as:

- You have the ability to properly regulate your emotions.
- You continue to have and pursue your own goals and dreams.
- You have a sense of purpose and are aware of your own significance.
- You can effectively communicate your needs.
- You are at ease with bonding with others,

closeness, and mutual reliance.

Now that you have a better understanding of attachment styles, you can do some introspection to determine which one you most closely identify with; this will bring you one step closer to healing any abandonment issues you may be experiencing.

Speaking of abandonment issues, let us take a look at some indicators that you should be on the lookout for that serve as strong indicators that you may need to make some changes.

Abandonment Issue Indicators

If you notice a pattern with any of the following indicators, it is time to step back and work on developing a healthier, more secure attachment style.

Too Close Too Soon

If you notice yourself attaching to people unusually quickly, you should question this aspect of yourself because it could be an indication of abandonment issues.

This may entail, among other things, acting like you are best friends or a couple too soon in the relationship or wanting to be with the other person all the time.

The other person in the relationship may feel suffocated by this conduct, withdraw, and act in the complete opposite way of what you had anticipated— acceptance, love, and caring.

Remaining in Abusive Relationships

You do not need a bigger indicator than this to know if you are dealing with abandonment issues: unhealthy and abusive relationships.

Because there is a deep-seated fear that you will not be loved and accepted by another person, staying in a destructive situation appears to be a delusional option that appears far better than experiencing abandonment.

Insecurity

When it comes to being a victim of emotional abuse, it is no secret that one of the most critical consequences is a lack of self-esteem.

When combined with the abuser's constant bombardment of delusions, the insecurity created makes it extremely difficult to make independent decisions with conviction and confidence. You can easily gauge this by paying attention to how you speak to yourself. Do you ever call yourself stupid or ugly for instance?

Trust Issues

Holding back emotionally and not being willing to open up and show vulnerability towards others are signs that you find it difficult to rely on or trust others.

Now, we do not have to go out and trust every single soul that crosses our paths, but opening up to others is not just about sharing our emotions, it also gives us a sense of belonging. With regard to abandonment, these trust issues are shrouded in suspicion and fear, causing you to feel defensive and constantly on guard.

Self-Blame

Do you always blame yourself as the source of the problem when things go awry in your relationship?

The inability to be objective and factual, and failing to see things for how they truly are, reinforces the unhealthy belief that no one wants you and the belief that you are not good enough or worthy of a healthy relationship. Nobody is perfect, and we all make mistakes, but constantly blaming or punishing yourself and feeling guilty about things you are not responsible for is unhealthy.

Controlling Behavior

When it comes to relationships, there is love and then there is control. It is natural to want everything in your relationships to be perfect; we all do. However, we cannot control everything all of the time.

Running around and making sure everything is perfect all the time because you are afraid of being abandoned is a sure sign that you are dealing with abandonment issues. Controlling everything is not only suffocating, but it also does not reflect a healthy, balanced relationship. Make sure that you want to meet standards and keep others happy because you want to, because you can, and because you love them, not because you are scared that they might abandon you.

These are a few signs that you might have been impacted and are now coping with issues related to desertion. The unpleasant truth is that if you do not deal with these problems, they will form part of the foundation of any other relationships you have in the future. So, if you want to attract the type of relationships you want, you need to become the type of person you want to attract, get rid of the baggage, and travel lightly into the beautiful future that awaits you.

Let us take a look at how you can lighten your load when it comes to overcoming abandonment issues.

Abandon Abandonment

Abandonment leaves scars that require time, love, and care to fully heal. As you have noticed from prior reading, abandonment issues can make you appear suspicious, paranoid, and needy, leaving you open to further mistreatment and abuse.

As with anything that needs to be healed, you must dig deep to find the root cause of the problem; otherwise, you will waste your precious energy treating symptoms rather than truly healing. As if dealing with the symptoms is not bad enough, being saddled with yet another partner who is wrong for you and repeating abusive cycles is not healthy either.

Here are some steps you can take to start changing

your mind and your behavior, which will yield better results than the terrible self-fulfilling prophecy known as abandonment issues.

Own It

To fully accept the problem, you must first recognize and acknowledge it. Name it, face it, declare that you have been betrayed, that you have been abandoned.

Take note of the emotions you are experiencing concerning the incidents, name them, and write them down. However, refrain from instilling any negative self-talk, such as self-blame.

Let Them Be

Do not try to hide any of the evoked emotions; it is critical that you experience them in order to release them.

Recognize them while also allowing yourself time to properly grieve the situation. It is simply a transition period that will assist you in moving in the right direction. Take it one step at a time, day by day.

You Are Not the Problem

A major sticking point with abandonment issues is having the notion that you are not lovable.

The important thing to remember is that you were not abandoned because you deserved it. There are things we can control, and then there are things we cannot, and being abandoned is most emphatically not one of the latter. It is also not your fault.

Establish Safe Relationships

Abuse, neglect, instability, or any other form of extensive trauma in a close relationship is synonymous with abandonment anxiety.

Healing properly will almost certainly require you to reach out, invest in, and nurture relationships with people who will appreciate, support, and respect you and facilitate you in forming secure attachment bonds. When it comes to relationships, you have options, and having safe, secure relationships is entirely possible.

Healthy Outlets

You must express yourself, let it all out, and channel those emotions into something that will benefit you psychologically.

You do not have to move mountains; it could be as simple as talking to a trusted friend, journaling, drawing, or trying out a new physical activity.

Ask for Help

Being able to ask for help is a very courageous thing to do, and we all need a little extra help from time to time.

Why not reach out and speak with a qualified therapist if it can help speed up your healing process, or how about joining a support group? Accept and make use of the fact that you have so many wonderful options at your disposal to help you regain your self-confidence, heal your self-esteem, and rebuild your trust in the world around you.

Healing from trauma and emotional abuse is not easy; it is a time-consuming process, but one thing is certain: It is well worth it, and with healing comes happiness. The best thing you can do is arm yourself with as much information as possible to combat these inner demons and scars, followed by action.

Now that we have looked in depth at many aspects of the effects of trauma and emotional abuse, let us focus on further healing and fostering happy relationships.

CHAPTER 10
BUILDING HEALTHIER RELATIONSHIPS

W e are all social creatures, no matter how much of a recluse you consider yourself to be. Being loved, accepted, and having a sense of belonging are not only some of the most precious things anyone can experience, but it is a right.

Not only does being loved and appreciated make you happy and give you a fulfilling existence, but studies have shown that it is also beneficial to your health and longevity (Umberson & Karas Montez, 2010). It is pivotal to be realistic and remember that relationships are not all moonlight and roses, they have their ups and downs. What matters is how each partner approaches and deals with these aspects, both positive and negative.

Both must strive to maintain and continuously develop the relationship; both must put forth the effort to make it work.

Let us start by looking at what a healthy relationship

looks like.

Is it Healthy?

Now that we know what an unhealthy relationship looks like in detail, we can ask what a healthy relationship looks like. What are the distinguishing features? What signs should you be on the lookout for?

So, let us get this party started with some more questions. Consider the following questions, whether you are in a relationship or it is still in its early stages:

- Is there mutual trust?
- Are we supportive of each other's interests?
- Do we have mutual respect for one another?
- Do we still have our individual identities?
- Do we freely express our feelings and thoughts to one another?
- Is our relationship based on equality and fairness?
- Are we affectionate towards each other?

These questions are based on some of the most important aspects of any relationship, whether it is between friends, family, or romantic partners. They indicate whether or not there is trust, respect, value, support, and honesty.

Let us focus on the factors that indicate whether you are in a healthy relationship.

Affection

Having fondness and affection for each other is a

distinguishing feature of a healthy relationship. Now, in romantic relationships, there is the infamous and much-loved "honeymoon phase" in which couples are completely enthralled with each other.

Yes, the breaks come and the initial intensity of all the fantastic emotions lessens with time, but this does not mean you no longer require tenderness, comfort, affection, or any of the other lovely experiences. In fact, the levels of emotional intimacy in healthy relationships deepen over time, as the initial passionate love starts to give way to compassionate love.

Mutual Respect

Healthy relationships are most definitely not characterized by acts of contempt or dismissal toward one another; rather, they are characterized by empathy, support, and trust, all contributing to building mutual respect.

This is displayed in different ways, through actions used to build each other up. It could include understanding, forgiveness, appreciating each other's individuality, showing interest and encouraging each other's passions and pursuits, and another important aspect: showing gratitude.

Reciprocity

Yes, you guessed it: Healthy relationships are all about giving and taking. This is not something that should be regularly updated on a sort of scoreboard to ensure that the scales are balanced.

You may need to give more than you take at times, and vice versa, depending on what each partner requires and the roles they play in the relationship. Some partners may be more like caregivers, while others may be like providers; this is not the end of the world; as long as everyone is happy and it is a healthy dynamic, everything should be fine.

Clear Communication

Communication, clarity, and respect are essential in any relationship, and this rule applies even when disagreements and arguments arise.

It does not matter if you have disagreements or arguments in your relationships, this is natural; what matters is how you resolve these issues and move forward. Do you still care about and respect one another? Is it more about finding a solution that benefits both parties than about who wins and who loses?

It is more important to solve problems in relationships than to avoid them as a way to maintain peace. Contrary to popular belief, research has shown that having conflict in relationships and constructively resolving it allows couples to positively build on the future of their relationships (Overall & McNulty, 2017).

Intimacy

Intimacy does not only refer to having a fantastic sex life with your partner; it also refers to things like holding hands, spending time alone, drowning in each other's eyes, building trust, and feeling safe.

In a relationship, intimacy is the establishment of a very close bond across all boards that comprise a relationship, and it is ultimately what distinguishes a relationship from a friendship.

Understanding that these aspects do exist in relationships is important because it allows you to make better decisions for yourself when it comes to forming bonds with others, knowing what will be beneficial to both you and the other party involved.

Let us take a look at some relationship tips to help you further nurture these beautiful aspects and fortify your bonds.

Better Building for Better Bonding

Relationships require work all of the time. It is all about creating positive habits and patterns to form a strong foundation for a healthy relationship, just as it is with you as an individual.

Once a positive, healthy foundation has been established, you can build on it to ensure that your relationship continues to grow and flourish into the bond of love and care that you deserve.

Firstly, Love Yourself

Self-love is not always easy to practice, especially for those who are or have been victims of abuse in any form.

However, it is necessary when it comes to being a part of a healthy relationship for the simple reason that you will attract what you project. Consider this: If you are a mental mess, lacking self-love and self-esteem, you will most likely attract someone who is either the same or who will step in and exploit your weaknesses. You will attract positive like-minded people if you have a strong sense of self and know what you want. After all, like attracts like, right?

You have the ability to rewrite your story and live the happy, fulfilled life you deserve.

Mutual Growth

It is time to alter our perspective on problems because, without them, we will not evolve and grow.

Problems force us out of our comfort zones and expose us to new, creative ways of thinking; instead, they should be viewed as opportunities that propel us forward and allow us to grow. And what better way to do it than with a loving, trusting partner?

Do not allow fear or the illusion of a perfect peaceful relationship free of obstacles to prevent you and your partner from growing in your relationship. You are there to support each other and grow together in the first place.

Honesty

Remember that "charity starts at home", and the same is true for the positive aspects of a relationship.

If you want love, you must first love yourself; if you want compassion, you must have self-empathy; and if you want honesty, you must be true, confident, and honest within yourself.

It is critical to approach every aspect of your relationship with honesty, including not running away from potential issues such as conflicts. Whether you are going through ups or downs, one of your greatest strengths will be your ability to weather the storm with honesty.

Appreciate the Differences
Instead of wanting to change a partner to be more like yourself, you should want to be with the person you fell in love with in the first place, not someone who has been panel-beaten into becoming a completely different being.

Appreciate their different approaches, and try to understand their various perspectives; you might learn a lot, and it also keeps things in your relationship interesting. You will be able to fully appreciate the relationship if you appreciate each other and foster individuality.

Up Those Standards
Just as your boundaries, you should never drop your standards. People with healthy standards are involved in healthy relationships.

If you do not have healthy standards, you are

allowing yourself to settle for less than you deserve. Do not back down from what you want out of a relationship, the type of partner you want, and what you need to feel physically and emotionally fulfilled.

Remember that the standard you set for others is the standard you must live by and pass on to others.

Focus Goes Where Energy Flows

Now, how will you spend your time and energy in your relationship? Is it better to focus on what is flawed or on the beauty and love that surrounds you?

Concentrate on healthy outcomes, solutions, and growth. If your focus is on finding a solution rather than the problem, your outcome will be growth, for example. Again, if you focus on appreciating differences rather than trying to change each other, you will grow and find joy and excitement.

Focusing your energy and channeling it into the right things will provide you with clarity and a healthy commitment.

Aligning Values

Values and goals differ from person to person, regardless of whether they are in relationships or not.

People in healthy relationships generally tend to have similar values, but differences can emerge over time, and yes, this is another common aspect of being in a relationship. Do not be concerned if you encounter any misalignments; the goal is to find a solution, a common ground where both parties can happily move forward. It is not about imposing your ideals on each other; rather, it should be viewed as an opportunity to learn, evolve, and grow as a couple.

Nurture Intimacy

It is all about the small moments in life, and it is the same when it comes to intimacy.

It is more than just being sexually intimate; it is about doing small things for each other, such as cooking a favorite meal, spending time together doing nothing, whether you are laying in bed or watching a movie, and sharing thoughts and emotions. Intimacy is all about the little details that happen to keep that spark alive.

Yes, it will take effort and attention to tend to each other's needs, but giving and receiving in this aspect is one of the most fulfilling experiences you will have.

Meeting Needs

Caring for and understanding each other's needs in a relationship is what leads to fulfillment. What more do you want than to see the person you care about happy and to have them want the same for you?

When it comes to meeting needs in a relationship, you must first understand what is required in order to fulfill all the core needs involved. Is it comfort, perhaps security? How should these needs be met, is it through communication, spending more time together, gifts of appreciation, or physical touch?

Are your requirements being met? You will need to develop a more emotional understanding that goes beyond the physical and intellectual. This is about understanding what the other person requires to feel fulfilled and how you can provide them with it. And, of course, this is a reciprocal aspect, as are all of these aspects in a healthy relationship.

Here you have it, a fantastically powerful package that you can use as a springboard to begin investing in more healthy, fulfilling relationships. All of this may appear to be logical, and it is. However, putting them into action is a completely different story. You must be aware of not only your partner's emotions and needs, but also your own, and work constantly to cultivate and grow these aspects to build a happy, healthy relationship.

Another crucial point to remember is that you have choices. You have the ability to choose what you focus on in a relationship, how you approach obstacles, and even whether the relationship is healthy and provides you with the components you need to live a fulfilled life. Remember that we must always grow and evolve; it is a necessary part of life, and if we are not growing, whether single or in a relationship, we are dying. As a result, do not back down from what you deserve; instead, keep moving forward, focusing on fulfillment.

Let us take a look at some exercises that you can

incorporate into your daily schedule that will work wonders on your journey of healing.

CHAPTER 11
HEALING IN PRACTICE

D o you truly understand what it means to say, "I need to heal and work on myself"?

We are all guilty of throwing these words around as if the changes we want to see are as superficial as making the statement. Working on yourself is a very important thing that should not be taken lightly; it can transform your life if done with sincere intent.

To heal, you must first have a genuine acceptance and understanding of what you have been through, be fully conscious of the impact it has had on you, and, most importantly, recognize that you have what it takes within you to bring about the necessary changes and step into your power. Again, easier said than done, is it not? Indeed, because this is a process that will require patience, dedication, and perseverance, it is sometimes easier for people to play the avoidance card and pretend that these things never happened or that they are not truly affected.

But this is not a healthy choice, and it is not the decision you want to make, because true joy exists, and we all deserve to experience it in all of its splendor. Healing does not imply that what you have gone through or the pain you have felt will magically disappear; rather, it means that it will no longer control you, and you will learn to take from it what you need to empower yourself and move forward. You will realize that what happened does not define you as a person, but rather the actions you take in response to it are what defines you.

Let us move forward and alter your perspective of pain so that you can undergo significant change, reclaim your value and self-worth, and live the life you deserve.

Self-Acceptance

Understanding and accepting your worth, regardless of whether you make mistakes or not, is what it means to value yourself. Your value is independent of other people's approval or other variables; it does not reside in a list of accomplishments, or a wall covered in certificates from floor to ceiling.

Reframing Self-Description

Simply put, stop judging yourself. Be more conscious of your self-perception, flaws, and all. Focus on your inner dialogue and self-talk, and alter how you describe yourself. Keep it impartial; there is no need to be dramatic or embellish the substitutes.

Exercise
1. Negative self-description: I am ugly.
2. Positive self-description replacement: Even if I do not always feel attractive, I am an irreplaceable, one-of-a-kind individual, and I matter.

Accepting Your Physical Appearance

Nobody is completely satisfied with their physical appearance, so it is natural to want to change certain physical aspects of yourself; it is human nature. Thus, the goal here is to learn to accept the physical aspects of yourself that cannot be changed. You are permitted to examine yourself, but only in a calm, non-judgmental manner.

Exercise
1. Stand in front of the mirror and give yourself a good, long look.
2. Concentrate on the aspects that you consider to be your flaws.
3. This may be difficult at first, but it will become easier with time.
4. Spend time on each aspect and examine it impartially.
5. Ask yourself objectively what it is about this aspect that you dislike.
6. With time this will teach you to accept yourself unconditionally.

Change Your Attitude

Accepting your flaws or mistakes without judging yourself is important in fostering self-value, not only for generating a more understanding approach towards yourself, but also for approaching these mistakes with curiosity and without judgment, allowing you to see where you went wrong and how you can improve.

This is a simple exercise; all you have to do is understand the three ways that humans react to failure, and by being aware of all the available options, you will be aware of your response. As a result of this awareness, you will be able to become more responsive rather than reactive.

Exercise

- Denial or defensiveness occurs when you minimize or ignore your mistakes. The avoidance of accepting responsibility for your actions is motivated by shame or the belief that you are unforgivable.
- Self-condemnation occurs when you fail to recognize that making mistakes is a natural part of life and that perfection, particularly when it comes to humans, does not exist. Failure to recognize this fact exposes you to an onslaught of self-loathing.
- Non-judgmental acceptance is what you want to do when you make a mistake. Acknowledge your shortcomings and mistakes, accept them, and move forward.

Self-Understanding

It is a strange phenomenon in our world that many people know their friends, family, or significant others better than they know themselves. It goes without saying that the better you understand yourself, the better you will be able to correct the aspects of your life that require positive change.

Let us proceed.

Build Your Picture

To begin, use the following simple exercise to draw a picture of yourself in order to better understand yourself. You can always go back to it and add to or adjust it as you grow and mold into the best version of yourself.

Exercise

1. Determine your most important values and characteristics: List five characteristics that you want to represent the way you want to live. Assertiveness, awareness, honesty, humor, musical abilities, networking, or becoming more physically active are examples of such traits. It could be anything you want to incorporate into your new life script.
2. Ask yourself what kind of person you want to be: You could begin by questioning yourself on how you think you come across to others, whether you are living in accordance with your values, and even what you perceive to be your strengths and weaknesses.
3. Create a character sketch of yourself: List all of

your positive qualities from the perspective of a third party. This will help you avoid being too judgmental towards yourself and instead see them as objective tools that contribute to your overall character.

Face Your Fear

Here is one truth: We will always be judged by others, whether we are delivering a profound speech or simply walking to the corner store. But we do not have to accept other people's opinions and perceptions of us. However, having low self-esteem can make this a real fear for some because they are afraid of being rejected and thought of as foolish.

You can counteract these notions with a simple exercise known as graded exposure. This method gradually exposes you to what you are attempting to avoid or fear, gradually desensitizing you to it and lessening the negative effects it has on you.

Exercise

1. Write down a list of everything that you fear and that causes you to engage in avoidance behavior.
2. Make a list of behaviors that you can use to counteract or alternate the avoidance behaviors.
3. If you: Avoid meeting new people because you are afraid of what they will think of you.
4. You could: Go out and meet people in smaller groups for shorter periods of time.
5. If you: Find it difficult to communicate in

social situations.

6. You could: Make it a point to say something to at least one person in the social setting.

7. Keep it simple to avoid feeling overwhelmed; the goal is to gradually reintroduce and integrate yourself into becoming less fearful.

Keep a Journal

Journaling appears frequently in this book because it is such an effective tool for inner reflection, allowing you to connect with yourself and become more self-aware, which is one of the most powerful ways to confront and change your inner critic.

Exercise

1. Set aside 10 minutes per day for two weeks to journal.

2. Make a list of everything you experience, including your thoughts and feelings, reflections, wishes, and concerns. It is not a test, so be open and honest, and write it down as it comes to you.

3. Review your entries weekly. See if you can identify any patterns in the emotions and thoughts you were having.

4. Examine why you made those entries, pay attention to the time and what happened, and you might notice some triggers or negative self-talk patterns. Try not to leave any stone unturned when it comes to where, what, why, how, who, and when.

5. Pay attention to what you are writing and saying to yourself after these reflection sessions, challenge the pitfalls, negative

patterns, and triggers that you have become aware of, and consciously replace them with positive reinforcements.

Self-Value

It all comes down to self-esteem. Yes, some folks are deemed to have a healthy supply of this while others find themselves on the other end of the spectrum, falling short of this important aspect of the "self".

Whatever caused your low self-esteem, the wonderful thing is that it can be built upon and improved. Let us take a look at some possible approaches.

Acknowledge Your Positive Aspects

We can all so easily fall into that horrible abyss of self-judgment, and before we know it, all we see about ourselves are our flaws. This is most emphatically not a healthy approach, so it is time to actively begin focusing on all the positive aspects of yourself and learn to embrace them.

Exercise

1. Reflect on your own strengths and write them down. If you are having difficulty seeing these aspects within yourself, you can Google personality strengths and see which ones resonate with you the most from the list. It does not matter if you are humble, loyal, moral, or creative; it is all about positivity, no matter how big or small.

2. Write five positive, truthful statements about yourself beneath your list of strengths. For instance, you could write that you are a supportive person to others, that you are a great listener, or that you are very responsible when it comes to meeting your responsibilities.
3. Once you have finished this, go over it carefully and think about every detail. Say them out loud and use them as mantras.
4. Repeat this reflection for several consecutive days to start establishing those new neural pathways.

Challenge Your Beliefs

How do you put something to the test? You begin by questioning it. Examine your beliefs to see which ones are holding you back. This will help you zero in on the aspects of your life that are impeding you from seeing yourself positively.

Exercise

1. Begin by identifying any limiting or negative beliefs you have. Perhaps you believe you are unworthy of love and a happy relationship. What limiting beliefs are you holding that are harming you?
2. Next, once you have established one, and only start with one, you can work your way through all of them one at a time, question yourself further.
3. What would be a better belief to hold than this one? Perhaps you believe that everyone deserves to be loved.
4. How would this new belief help you in

comparison to the old one you were clinging to? For example, you could close your eyes and observe how it alters your perspective.

5. What are the potential drawbacks in comparison to the old belief?

Positive Personal Affirmations

This is a simple daily exercise that you can do, no matter where you are or what you are doing, to help you develop a strong, distinct positive self-identity. It is as simple as creating personal affirmations that resonate with you and making an effort to regularly repeat them.

Exercise

1. Take some time to think about positive affirmations that you can relate to and that are unique to you.
2. Place these affirmations somewhere you will see them regularly so they serve as constant reminders.
3. Here are some examples:
    a. I could deal with adversity and rejection because they are simply redirection and protection.
    b. I value my individuality; I am one of a kind.
    c. I can make fun of myself.
    d. I am deserving of love, happiness, and fulfillment.
4. You can write anything that your heart desires to embrace and improve upon yourself.

Self-Care

Your physical health is just as crucial to living a fulfilled life as your mental health. If your body is ignored, it is impossible to feel good.

People frequently link physical health to eating well and working out consistently, overlooking the significance of brain health in the process. Here we will look at some factors for consideration concerning your physical health.

Follow a Healthy Diet

You are probably well aware that you should consume all of your vegetables and restrict your intake of sweets and processed foods. After all, most of us have internalized this since childhood, and for a good cause, of course.

One suggestion is to evaluate your eating practices and food standards using the Mediterranean diet. It is abundant in anti-inflammatory agents, nutrients, minerals, and vitamins that are best for physical well-being, including omega-3, which is strongly advised for brain health.

Tips

- Eat mostly natural plant-based foods and try to avoid processed foods like cakes, ready-made meals, and takeaways as much as possible.
- Make sure you get enough high-quality proteins in your diet, such as eggs, beans, legumes, and oily fish.

- Limit your consumption of red meat, particularly processed meats such as corned beef or ham.
- Pay attention to how your meals are prepared, whether you eat out or at home try to avoid deep-fried foods as much as possible.
- Pay attention to the fats you consume, making sure you stick to unsaturated fats that are available in olive oil, seeds, fish, and nuts for instance.

Regular Physical Activity

Aside from feeling as fit as a fiddle and looking great, regular physical activity is a great way to alleviate stress and improve mental health.

Tips

- If you are not physically active, begin slowly and gradually increase your activity level as your fitness levels improve.
- To maintain overall health, it is recommended that a person engages in at least 45 minutes of regular physical activity three to five times per week (The Lancet, 2018).
- Choose activities that you enjoy doing; it is not meant to feel like a chore, but rather provide you with a sense of relief and improved health.
- If you are taking any medications or have any serious health conditions, you should consult with your doctor before beginning any physical regimen.

Get Proper Sleep

Proper sleep does not simply refer to getting enough sleep; rather, it is about quality as well as quantity. Have you ever heard of the term "sleep hygiene"? This refers to getting enough, regular, and high-quality sleep.

Tips

- Sleep quality: Make your bedroom a relaxing haven where you can unwind and get the rest you require. Avoid using technology, bright lights, and loud noises in your bedroom. Make sure your bedroom temperature is not too hot or too cold, and develop a sleep routine that includes retiring for the day and removing all distractions for at least an hour before going to bed.

- The right amount of sleep: There is such a thing as too little sleep and too much sleep, neither of these are healthy and conducive to improving mood and performance. You will need between seven and eight hours of uninterrupted sleep a night to enable your body to fully recover and recharge.

- Regular sleep: Do your best to maintain a regular sleeping schedule. To help ensure the consistency of your body's essential sleep cycle, try to go to bed and wake up at the same time each day. Because your body recovers and recharges throughout the sleep cycle, regularly disturbing it puts you at risk for a variety of health issues, including insomnia, tiredness, and lack of concentration, to mention a few.

Self-Empowerment

If you could only use one word to empower yourself, what do you think it would be?

Assertiveness.

Being assertive gives you the strength to express your wants, feelings, and thoughts in a positive, self-assured way without exaggerating your own capabilities, while also allowing others the freedom to do the same with their thoughts, feelings, and needs. Let us look at some steps you can start employing in becoming more assertive.

Exercise

1. When you are in a position where you feel like you need to speak up, do it in the most factual manner possible without losing your composure and getting overly emotional.
2. Nobody can read minds, so try to be as clear as you can in describing your viewpoint. Clearly state what you would like to achieve from your end.
3. Give the other person a chance to express their viewpoint, and when they do, respond with understanding rather than hostility.
4. Try to come up with potential solutions that will not jeopardize the happiness of any parties involved once everyone has voiced their concerns.

These are merely a few easy activities you could start using to promote healing. It is crucial to understand that recovery requires time and patience in order to replace many of the damaging messages that have been ingrained in us throughout our lives, whether by ourselves or other people.

We have discussed various approaches to healing from emotional abuse and trauma up to this point, but before we conclude, let us take a closer look at the various stages of healing.

CHAPTER 12
HEALING STAGES

W hen you reach this point, it means that you have decided that enough is enough and that you are reclaiming your right to live a happy and fulfilled life.

This is not an easy decision to make; after all, you are leaving someone you have not only grown accustomed to but also genuinely loved, and perhaps still do. This is most likely one of the most courageous things you could do for yourself. But now what? What can you expect in the midst of all the knowledge, exercises, devastation, confusion, and relief?

You should begin by understanding that not all good changes are easy and that your life has not fallen apart; rather, it is just getting started. Of course, you have a lot of questions, so let us start by looking at the various stages of healing to broaden your knowledge of the subject.

Stages of Healing

When it comes to the healing process, there are typically five stages (Gavin, 1988). Because everyone is unique, the lengths of each stage may vary, and occasionally they may even coexist. So, keep an open mind and only accept this as a general suggestion rather than a firm prognostication.

Denial and Grief

When it comes to relationships, grief occurs when you are lamenting a kind of loss, whether it was caused by rejection, abandonment, or your own decision to end the connection.

There is no getting around the fact that grief will exist and play a part in your recovery process, even if you were in the worst relationship ever. Before you can express your grief, you must first go through the process of acceptance. You must accept what has occurred to you. Denial is another challenging obstacle to overcome. With time, this defense mechanism that is activated in an effort to shield ourselves from emotional anguish will also subside, making room for acceptance.

Anger

You will undoubtedly feel angry after accepting denial and grief. You must again navigate this phase, by recognizing and properly channeling your anger into healthy endeavors you will speed up the process, bringing you closer to brighter days.

Negotiation

This is probably one of the stages where most people give up and turn around, so be wary.

There is a lot of self-talk and negotiating during this phase. Perhaps if you both seek help and counseling, the abuser will change; perhaps if you had done things differently, things would have turned out differently; or perhaps if you go back and try again, you will be able to change this person. It is critical to follow your head rather than your heart, but more on that with further reading.

Depression

When you start to realize what you have been through, it can be overwhelming and emotionally draining, sending you into a depressive spiral.

When you feel your self-worth has been depleted, you tend to withdraw as you enter one of the most difficult stages of the healing process. It is important to note that if you are having difficulty navigating the process, it is strongly advised that you seek help from a qualified therapist as soon as possible.

Acceptance

This stage is frequently misunderstood as a great moment, but it is not.

When the pain has subsided and the struggle has begun to fade, it is similar to being in the eye of a storm. You have an unsettling calm brought on by your fears of what is to come. However, do not be discouraged, because this is also where the great turning point occurs, where hope and faith emerge, bringing forth new growth and your new life slowly unfolds as you build upon yourself.

Since you will now begin to have power over your life again, your decisions should be based on an awareness of how they will affect your recovery and help you become the person you want to be. Thus, a better understanding of how to navigate the actual healing process will help you accelerate your journey.

Helpful Healing Hints

Here are some very simple hints to keep in mind as you travel down the path of healing that you can pull out and use whenever the need arises.

Grieving Is Essential

Leaving any relationship is a difficult thing to do; in fact, they say that being separated from those we love could be akin to experiencing the death of a loved one at times.

It is critical to recognize the necessity to embrace these emotions; you must grieve your loss in order to progress to the next stage of your healing process. It is a natural part of creating a better future for yourself, getting rid of the old in order to make room for the new.

If you find yourself in these moments of despair, remember that this, too, shall pass and that when it does, things will only get better. Remind yourself of your future plans, your dreams, and how you will feel with your newfound independence and emotional freedom. Remember that you are gaining more than you are losing in this situation.

Treat Anxiety and Depression Immediately

It is critical to seek immediate professional help if you are experiencing any symptoms of PTSD, depression, or anxiety.

You are already in the midst of a healing process, and you do not need to add to the stress when any of these symptoms begin to spiral out of control and throw you into a deeper bout of despair. Getting the proper assistance and treatment as soon as possible should be high on your priority list, especially if it is something that is manageable or preventable.

Head Over Heart

Walking away from abusive relationships and staying away will require you to use your head rather than your heart when making decisions.

Your heart is filled with emotion, which can sometimes lead to irrational behavior, such as returning to your abuser because you believe true love deserves another chance. However, when you are emotionally vulnerable, it is not a good time to make decisions that should benefit your heart's interests.

You need to think logically and rationally, this is why you need to use your head. It is illogical to return to an abusive situation and deprive yourself of the opportunity to experience true love and joy. You need to move forward in a strategic fashion and the only thing that should be in your heart is your best interests.

Heal and Learn First

The aftermath of leaving an abusive relationship is depleting on so many levels, and not wanting to jump into a new relationship right away is quite normal.

Unfortunately, some people do not give this part of the process enough time. The problem with not giving yourself enough time to recover and heal is that you do not learn enough and may seek comfort in the same abusive patterns. Remember our discussion about like attracting like?

Channel Your Anger

Forget about smashing car windows and making public displays of rage; instead, keep your cool and channel your rage into things that will benefit you.

Join a karate club, take an art class, visit a therapist, or even punch your pillow. Being angry at yourself or your abuser, as well as harboring feelings of resentment, is another normal aspect of the healing process, but remember that things are getting better every day in every way. What is important is how you handle the situation. Will you be reactive or responsive?

Since you now have power over your life, your decisions should be based on an awareness of how they will affect your recovery and help you become the person you want to be.

We will all experience adversity in different ways and at different times in our life, but by understanding the stages of the healing process, you will be better equipped to effectively manage these challenges, stay on course, and emerge from the storm.

CONCLUSION

I hope this has changed your perspective so that the next time you hear the word "abuse" you will understand that it refers to both physical and emotional abuse. It does not imply that if there are no visible wounds and scars the person is not being abused.

While physical abuse leaves visible damage on its victims, emotional abuse is much harder to see, which makes it much more difficult to determine, even for those who succumb to it. Both of these incidents are extremely serious, causing such profound damage that the victims continue to suffer from deep emotional wounds even after the relationship has ended. If left unchecked, these abusive impacts can have a profound negative effect on your understanding of yourself and the world around you.

The abuser uses the heinous strategies we have discussed to undermine your sense of identity, self-worth, and independence in an effort to exert control over you. This horrible and entirely selfish strategy is reprehensible.

The most crucial thing you should understand and take to heart before you finish reading the last words in this book is that it is not your fault and you do not deserve to be treated this way under any circumstances. Every living person has the right to live a life filled with joy, accomplishments, and the realization of their dreams. We are all free individuals, and with that freedom comes the ability to choose. You have the right to make your own choices and decisions that will help you live the life you were born to live.

Your feelings and experiences are valid, and you should never try to downplay the gravity of what you have been through. Avoid this pitfall that, unfortunately, most victims fall into to protect the abuser, which is driven by feelings of guilt and shame, which are also the chains that keep most people tied to these destructive relationships.

The good news is that you have the ability to recover, separate, and reclaim your life. Many people have successfully left abusive relationships and made the transition from being victims to survivors, from being drained and dependent to being fulfilled and self-reliant. Would you like even more good news?

You already have what it takes within you to go through the same amazing transformation. After all, this is one of the first ways you empowered yourself, by arming yourself with knowledge through reading this book. Knowledge is power, especially when put into action.

You now have a better understanding of what emotional abuse is and how to recognize and heal from it. Your knowledge has grown by understanding narcissistic tactics, as well as how to spot these evils and successfully avoid them. Along with gaslighting and codependency, you are well-versed in post-traumatic stress disorder and its relationship to emotional abuse and trauma. Along with approaches to PTSD healing, you have been introduced to a variety of strategies for breaking free from unhealthy patterns and establishing proper boundaries in order to begin prioritizing yourself.

Yes, you should be your number one priority; this is not selfish, but rather realistic. We looked at obsessive thinking and abandonment fears, and how they stem from emotional abuse. You have been made aware as well of the different types of attachment styles, so keep an eye out for them in your relationships. Secure attachment styles are what we are aiming for in healthy relationships where all parties are respected, understood, loved, and cared for.

Then we got to the good stuff, which was all about focusing on the positive and learning about what happy, healthy relationships entail and how to foster them. It may be difficult for you to believe at times, but loving, fulfilling relationships do exist; they are not the stuff of fairy tales, and you most certainly deserve to experience them. You also have some fantastic exercises that you can begin incorporating into your daily routine to aid in your healing. Keep in mind to be patient and consistent. In a year, one small step per day will add up to an entire journey of change; every little bit of effort and care you put into yourself will most certainly be worthwhile in the end.

We discussed healing and the stages to expect, as well as some helpful hints to help you better navigate these stages. Remember that the day you make the conscious decision to take the first step and reclaim your life, regardless of the ups and downs you will face, you are healing, and you are one step closer to being the best version of yourself and living the fulfilled life you deserve.

It is time to stop looking back and reject the distorted reality that emotional abuse and trauma have imposed on you. Nobody has the power to control your life; it is a gift that each of us has been given; simply giving this power to the likes of an abuser is not what it was intended for. Aside from the fact that they should never be given the privilege, they are simply not worth the time and effort you could put into yourself and other healthy relationships where your mere presence would bring a smile to the faces of others.

You know enough to get the ball rolling with all of

the ins and outs of these abusive tactics used to manipulate and control you. Use this knowledge and information as part of your arsenal when it comes to putting your foot down and saying enough is enough. I will reiterate that the other important aspect of your healing is to build a strong supportive network around you. This may be one of the most difficult things to do at first, but you will be pleasantly surprised at how much support you will receive and may end up wondering why you did not take these steps sooner.

This brings me to my final breath; healing is different for everyone. There is no set period of time; the only thing that exists is the time you have right now and what you choose to do with it. In order to contribute to others in a healthy manner and live a life full of love, make sure you use this time to fill your own cup to the point of overflow.

Remember, you already have what it takes to transform from victim to survivor within you; it is time to wake up from this nightmare and step into your dream life.

FREE GIFT

Greetings!

First of all, we want to thank you for reading our books. We aim to create the very best books for our readers.

Now we invite you to join our exclusive list. As a subscriber, you will receive a free gift, weekly tips, free giveaways, discounts and so much more.

All of this is 100% free with no strings attached!

To claim your bonus simply head to the link below or scan the QR code below.

RELOVEPSYCHOLOGY

https://www.subscribepage.com/relovepsychology

REFERENCES

Abraham, M. (2022, September 6). How to Stop Obsessive Thoughts and Anxiety.CalmClinic https://www.calmclinic.com/anxiety/signs/obsessive-thoughts

American Psychiatric Association. (2019). Get Help With PTSD. Psychiatry.org. https://www.psychiatry.org/patients-families/ptsd

American Psychological Association. (n.d.). APA Dictionary of Psychology. Dictionary.apa.org. Retrieved January 9, 2023, from https://dictionary.apa.org/codependency

Arzt, N. (2022, November 25). 15 Tips for Recovering from Narcissistic Abuse. Choosing Therapy. https://www.choosingtherapy.com/recovering-from-narcissistic-abuse/

Attachment Project, The. (2020, July 2). Secure Attachment: The 5 Conditions Required for Every Child. https://www.attachmentproject.com/blog/secure-attachment/

Beau, A. (2021, October 8). 6 Mantras to Help You Prioritize Yourself and Your Needs. Shine. https://advice.theshineapp.com/articles/6-mantras-to-help-you-prioritize-yourself-and-your-needs/

Bennett, T. (2018, April 2). Healing from Abandonment: 5 Pieces of Advice That Light the Way. Thriveworks. https://thriveworks.com/blog/healing-abandonment-advice-light-way/

Burch, K. (2022, December 3). How to Recognize the Signs of Narcissistic Abuse. Verywell Health. https://www.verywellhealth.com/narcissistic-abuse-5220194

Campbell, L. (2021, June 8). Personal Boundaries: Types and How to Set Them. Psych Central. https://psychcentral.com/lib/what-are-personal-boundaries-how-do-i-get-some

Cherry, K. (2022, February 21). Are You In a Healthy Relationship? Verywell Mind. https://www.verywellmind.com/all-about-healthy-relationship-4774802#citation-1

Codependency. (2022). Psychology Today https://www.psychologytoday.com/us/basics/codependency

Davenport, B. (2022, August 27). 7 Stages Of Healing From Emotional Abuse. Live Bold and Bloom. https://liveboldandbloom.com/08/emotional-abuse/healing-from-emotional-abuse

Davies, D. S. (2019, August 17). Narcissistic Abuse & the Drama Triangle. drsarahdavies.com. https://www.drsarahdavies.com/post/narcissistic-abuse-the-drama-triangle

Degges-White, S. (2022, December 9). Gaslighting Behavior Is a Sign of Weakness. Psychology Today. https://www.psychologytoday.com/us/blog/lifetime-connections/202212/gaslighting-behavior-is-a-sign-of-weakness

Dibdin, E. (2022, April 11). 9 Ways to Cope With Intrusive Thoughts. Psych Central. https://psychcentral.com/health/ways-to-let-go-of-stuck-thoughts#what-are-intrusive-thoughts

Farlex. (n.d.). TheFreeDictionary.com. Retrieved January 9, 2023, from https://medical-dictionary.thefreedictionary.com/abuse

Firestone, L. (2017, August 17). The Unselfish Art of Prioritizing Yourself. Psychology Today. https://www.psychologytoday.com/us/blog/compassion-matters/201708/the-unselfish-art-prioritizing-yourself

Gaslighting. (2022). Psychology Today. https://www.psychologytoday.com/us/basics/gaslighting

Gavin, P. E. (1988). Five Stages of Healing. Gavin & Dersch Law and Mediation. https://www.gavinfamilylaw.com/articles-and-resources/five-stages-of-healing/

Gillihan, S. J. (2019, April 26). How to Recover From Gaslighting. WebMD. https://blogs.webmd.com/from-our-archives/20190426/how-to-recover-from-gaslighting

Goldberg, H. (2018, February 13). You Are Your Most Important Relationship. Shine. https://advice.theshineapp.com/articles/how-to-prioritize-your-most-important-relationship-yourself/?utm_source=Shine&utm_medium=Blog

Gordon, S. (2022b, January 5). What Is Gaslighting? Verywell Mind. https://www.verywellmind.com/is-someone-gaslighting-you-4147470

Gould, W. R. (2022, November 7). What Is Codependency? Verywell Mind. https://www.verywellmind.com/what-is-codependency-5072124#citation-1

Haupt, A. (2022, April 18). How to recognize gaslighting and respond to it. Washington Post. https://www.washingtonpost.com/wellness/2022/04/15/gaslighting-definition-relationship-abuse-response/

Huizen, J. (2022, July 14). What is gaslighting? Examples and how to respond. Medical News Today. https://www.medicalnewstoday.com/articles/gaslighting#how-it-works

Is Abuse Really a "Cycle"? (n.d.). National Domestic Violence Hotline. https://www.thehotline.org/resources/is-abuse-really-a-cycle/

Jones, H. (2022, September 13). How Do I Know If I'm In a Codependent Relationship? Verywell Health. https://www.verywellhealth.com/codependency-5093171

Karakurt, G., & Silver, K. E. (2013). Emotional abuse in intimate relationships: The role of gender and age. Violence and Victims, 28(5), 804–821. https://www.ncbi.nlm.nih.gov/pmc/articles/PMC3876290/

Kaszina, A. (2016, January 19). Emotional Abuse And Abandonment Revealed. Recoverfromemotionalabuse.com. https://recoverfromemotionalabuse.com/2016/01/emotional-abuse-and-abandonment/

Kelly, O. (2020, November 13). How OCD Can Cause Different Cognitive Distortions. Verywell Mind. https://www.verywellmind.com/cognitive-distortions-and-ocd-2510477

Kirk, I. (2009, July 2). Codependency - Good Or Bad? EzineArticles. https://ezinearticles.com/?Codependency---Good-Or-Bad?&id=2530211

Knapek, E., & Kuritárné Szabó, I. (2014). A kodependencia fogalma, tünetei és a kialakulásában szerepet játszó tényezők [The concept, the symptoms and the etiological factors of codependency]. Psychiatria Hungarica,, 29(1), 56–64. Hungarian. https://pubmed.ncbi.nlm.nih.gov/24670293/

Koutsimani, P., Montgomery, A., & Georganta, K. (2019). The Relationship Between Burnout, Depression, and Anxiety: A Systematic Review and Meta-Analysis. Frontiers in Psychology, 10(284). https://doi.org/10.3389/fpsyg.2019.00284

Kvarnstrom, E. (2018, January 16). Why Emotional Abuse Can Cause a Nervous Breakdown and How You Can Recover. Bridges to Recovery. https://www.bridgestorecovery.com/blog/emotional-abuse-can-cause-nervous-breakdown-can-recover/

Lancet, The. (2018, August 8). Exercise linked to improved mental health, but more may not always be better. ScienceDaily. https://www.sciencedaily.com/releases/2018/08/180808193656.htm

Loggins, B. (2021, November 22). Healing After Narcissistic Abuse: What Does Healing Look Like? Verywell Mind. https://www.verywellmind.com/stages-of-healing-after-narcissistic-abuse-5207997

Martin, S. (2022, October 22). 6 Tips for Ending a Cycle of Unhealthy Relationships. Psychology Today. https://www.psychologytoday.com/us/blog/conquering-codependency/202010/6-tips-ending-cycle-unhealthy-relationships

Michael, J. (2016, May 5). Prioritizing Yourself: 7 Ways to Incorporate Self-Care — Blog. Jody Michael Associates. https://www.jodymichael.com/blog/prioritizing-7-ways-incorporate-self-care/

Moore, M. (2022, September 8). Here's 3 Ways Boundaries Can Help You. Psych Central. https://psychcentral.com/relationships/the-importance-of-personal-boundaries#Lets-recap

Morin, A. (2021, July 30). Friday Fix: How to Break Free From Unhealthy Patterns. Verywell Mind. https://www.verywellmind.com/how-to-break-free-from-unhealthy-patterns-the-verywell-mind-podcast-episode-92-5194876

Neuharth, D. (2017, September 14). 14 Thought-Control Tactics Narcissists Use to Confuse and Dominate You. Psych Central. https://psychcentral.com/blog/narcissism-decoded/2017/09/14-thought-control-tactics-narcissists-use-to-confuse-and-dominate-you#1

Neuharth, D. (2021, March 9). 8 Insidious Ways Narcissists Try to Control You. Psychology Today. https://www.psychologytoday.com/us/blog/narcissism-demystified/202103/8-insidious-ways-narcissists-try-control-you

Obsessive Thinking: Worry and Rumination. (2022). Cognitive Health Group, PLLC. https://cognitive-behavior-therapy.com/cognitive-behavior-therapy-for-obsessive-thinking-worry-rumination

Overall, N. C., & McNulty, J. K. (2017). What type of communication during conflict is beneficial for intimate relationships? Current Opinion in Psychology, 13(13), 1–5. https://doi.org/10.1016/j.copsyc.2016.03.002

Pattemore, C. (2021, June 3). 10 Ways to Build and Preserve Better Boundaries. Psych Central. https://psychcentral.com/lib/10-way-to-build-and-preserve-better-boundaries#types

Peabody, K. (2022). 12 Types of Emotional Abuse That Aren't Physical Violence. The Therapy Group. https://www.thetherapygroup.com/thetherapygroupblog/12-types-of-emotional-abuse-that-arent-physical-violence

Pietrangelo, A. (2019b, March 29). What Are the Short- and Long-Term Effects of Emotional Abuse? Healthline. https://www.healthline.com/health/mental-health/effects-of-emotional-abuse

Pietrangelo, A., & Raypole, C. (2022, January 28). Emotional Abuse: What It Is and Signs to Watch For. Healthline. https://www.healthline.com/health/signs-of-mental-abuse#neglect-and-isolation

Rackliffe, C. (n.d.). 5 Ways to Heal a Fear of Abandonment. crackliffe.com https://www.crackliffe.com/words/2022/7/14/how-to-heal-fear-of-abandonment

Raypole, C. (2020a, March 30). 9 Tips for Narcissistic Abuse Recovery. Healthline. https://www.healthline.com/health/mental-health/9-tips-for-narcissistic-abuse-recovery

Raypole, C. (2020d, June 25). Think You're Being Gaslit? Here's How to Respond. Healthline. https://www.healthline.com/health/how-to-deal-with-gaslighting

Robbins, T. (2022). How to have a healthy relationship.

Tonyrobbins.com. https://www.tonyrobbins.com/ultimate-relationship-guide/healthy-relationship-you-deserve/

Sissons, B. (2022, October 5). Narcissistic abuse: Definition, signs, and recovery. Medical News Today. https://www.medicalnewstoday.com/articles/narcissistic-abuse#the-signs

Smith, S. (2019, June 6). How to Deal with Gaslighting in 6 Easy Steps. Marriage.com.. https://www.marriage.com/advice/mental-health/how-to-deal-with-gaslighting/

Smith, S. (2022, May 10). 15 Signs of Abandonment Issues and How to Deal With Them. Marriage.com. https://www.marriage.com/advice/mental-health/abandonment-issues/

Spinazzola, J. (2014). Childhood psychological abuse as harmful as sexual or physical abuse. American Psychological Association. https://www.apa.org/news/press/releases/2014/10/psychological-abuse

Stern, R., & Wolf, N. (2018). The gaslight effect: How to spot and survive the hidden manipulation others use to control your life. Harmony Books. (Original work published 2007)

Stines, Dr. S. (2017, December 20). Emotional Abuse and Threats of Abandonment. Psych Central. https://psychcentral.com/pro/recovery-expert/2017/12/emotional-abuse-and-threats-of-abandonment#4

Summersault, A. (2020, November 13). How To Break Out Of Unhealthy Relationship Patterns. Medium. https://medium.com/change-your-mind/how-to-break-out-of-unhealthy-relationship-patterns-f518d771cb0a

Sweet, P. L. (2019). The Sociology of Gaslighting. American Sociological Review, 84(5), 851–875. https://doi.org/10.1177/0003122419874843

Taylor, K. (2018, June 4). Tips to Overcome Abandonment Issues in Relationship. Marriage.com. https://www.marriage.com/advice/relationship/overcome-abandonment-issues/

Top 18 Self Esteem Exercises. (2022, September 11). Ineffableliving.com. https://ineffableliving.com/raising-low-self-esteem/

Umberson, D., & Karas Montez, J. (2010). Social relationships and health: A flashpoint for health policy. Journal of Health and Social Behavior, 51(suppl), S54–S66. https://doi.org/10.1177/0022146510383501

Valdez, R. (2021, December 21). Can Emotional Abuse Cause PTSD? Verywell Health. https://www.verywellhealth.com/ptsd-from-emotional-abuse-5210626

Wegner, D. M., Schneider, D. J., Carter, S. R., & White, T. L. (1987).

Paradoxical effects of thought suppression. Journal of Personality and Social Psychology, 53(1), 5-13.3. https://doi.org/10.1037/0022-3514.53.1.5

What Is Abuse? How Does It Happen? (2020, March 24). Domestic Violence: It's EVERYBODY'S Business. https://domesticviolence.org/what-is-abuse/

OTHER BOOKS BY
RELOVE PSYCHOLOGY

Available now in Ebook, Paperback and
Hardcover in all regions.

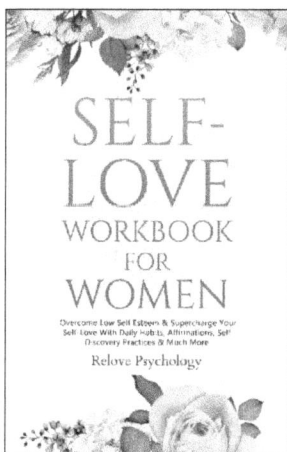

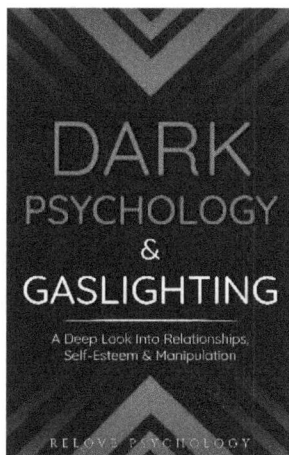

DARK PSYCHOLOGY & GASLIGHTING

We sincerely hope you enjoyed our new book **"Dark Psychology & Gaslighting"**. We would greatly appreciate your feedback with an honest review at the place of purchase.

First and foremost, we are always looking to grow and improve as a team. It is reassuring to hear what works, as well as receive constructive feedback on what should improve. Second, starting out as an unknown author is exceedingly difficult, and Amazon reviews go a long way toward making the journey out of anonymity possible. Please take a few minutes to write an honest review.

Best regards,
Relove Psychology
http://relovepsychology.com/

www.ingramcontent.com/pod-product-compliance
Lightning Source LLC
Chambersburg PA
CBHW060502030426
42337CB00015B/1702